0

Published by Aqeel Ash-Shakoor for

Mogul NstinQ, LLC.

Lansing, Michigan, USA

ISBN -13 978-0-692-39813-5

ISBN- 10 0-692-39813-9

No More Chains!

The Rule 2:22 Principle

~His Excellency Rev Dr. Aqeel T. Ash-Shakoor, CDKA~

ENDORSEMENTS

"Knowledge of the truth is the only road to true freedom. In this book, Dr. Ash-Shakoor shows you the road so you can move from prison to palace. He also gives you the hammer to break the chains that have been holding you from arriving at your palace. As you read and apply the content of this book, you will experience a new level of success."

Dr. Benson Agbortogo

Founder, Kingdom Embassy Network

ENDORSEMENTS

The Pharisees tried to put heavy burdens on God's people, like people in our lives today. Whether it's family, friends, associates, your job, finances, whatever the hindrance as we learn from Jesus.

Matthew 11:28-30 KJV 28) Come unto me, all ye that labour and are heavy laden, and I will give you rest. 29) Take my yoke upon you, and learn of me; for I am meek and lowly in heart: and ye shall find rest unto your souls. 30) For my yoke is easy, and my burden is light. ...

All of your heartaches, your pain, your worries, and your stresses, take it to Jesus! He will unloose the shackles of heart break, the shackles of disappointment, the shackles of sickness, the shackles of sadness, the shackles of unemployment, and the shackles of bad finances! Seek the kingdom of God, and watch the chains begin to fall and your yoke of bondage will be yoke of blessings, which in found in Christ Jesus!

His Excellency Rev. Dr. Aqeel Ash-Shakoor, CDKA addresses the problems of chains and yokes in which we have affixed ourselves to in the first segment of this great work. In the final segment, he delivers the powerful principle that should be used to break not only the physical chains and yokes but the psychological aspects. "No More Chains! The Rule 2:22 Principle" is arguably a thorough guide to jumpstarting a greater self-improvement. Dr. Ash-Shakoor creatively uses biblical principles of the Old and New Testament chapters and verses of 2:22 to lay the foundational work for assessing and resolving the problems of chains and yokes. He additionally supplies scholarly research to increase the awareness and make this work suitable for the average business person.

Easily a work that could have been two separate offerings, Dr. Ash-Shakoor supplies this two-in-one masterpiece to serve humanity with encouragement, exhortation, and uplift. He is arguably the anointed and creative mind that you must have instruct your next professional development training.

~Minister Michael V. Madric II

Praise Nation Ministries

"Education nurtures the hearts and minds of those, who have chosen not to follow, but to lead."

~Dr. Aqeel Taahir Ash-Shakoor, CDKA~

CONTENTS

CONTENTS

CONTENTS

"*You don't have to worry about what God has already given you, you just have to access the door God has opened for you! Stop begging for what's already yours!*"

~Dr. Aqeel Taahir Ash-Shakoor, CDKA~

PREFACE

I'm lamenting as I begin to pen this work because I love people. I literally have tears in my eyes because I know that this work is going to bless a multitude of people. I wish for you to have the greatness of all God has for you. I wish that I could tell you that I'm wealthy and never have problems but that's far from the truth. However, in order to relate to you I wrote from the heart giving you solutions to all our problems and issues. I'm just so thankful to Jesus that He used me in this awesome privilege to Encourage, Exhort, & Uplift you.

Your very first step to walking out of your chains was purchasing this work. Why you might ask, well if you only buy books because someone recommended them then you are still in chains. This means that you solely rely on others to tell you what books you should or shouldn't read. Maybe the person that referenced the types of books they read may have been further along in life if they did read other material than those he or she is familiar with. There just may have been that one nugget that was found in the third paragraph of the eighth chapter on page seventy something that would have the next level thought that one has been missing all their life, but now they will never receive it. Now as a preliminary, I would tell you to invest in knowledge that is intended to challenge your thinking if you wish to advance in life and not be stagnated.

"No More Chains! The Rule 2:22 Principle" is a progressive mindset. This proactive and progressive mindset is one that many of us lack or have developed due to the people, places, and things we have come in contact with. No one really likes to think they have been a follower but naturally we all follow something even when we choose to lead. However, those that choose to lead break off from the normalcy of all, part, or some previous patterns or thoughts that we ourselves had begun to follow.

This valuable chain or yoke breakers are essential to any reader or person seeking self and professional development. They can also become a practice collectively as well as individually for thriving companies, corporations, or organizations seeking to break their comfort levels or plateaus that would appear to be a glass ceiling. Most of what we see as a glass ceiling is because we refuse to change our mindsets or view of the glass ceiling. Sure it's a glass ceiling. Well now that you know it's a glass ceiling, you should take in consideration that glass ceilings are made of glass. Therefore as you probably have already figured out, "you can break through the glass." We've just been directly or indirectly trained to stop and only look through the glass like window shoppers.

"No More Chains! The Rule 2:22 Principle" works to break those commonplace chains that are so comfortable that keeps us in uncomfortable environments or positions. We generally have every answer that we seek but we also become the biggest obstacle we face in order to excel or progress in life. Self-improvement is realigning our thoughts just as well as ourselves to approach matters differently. Some may wish to relate this thinking to the glass being half full or half empty, but I rather think of what's the purpose or how can I use the glass whether its half full or half empty.

As you see, we are still dealing with the same object or subject but instead of seeing it for what it maybe, "No More Chains! The Rule 2:22 Principle" deals with combating the approach to how I can use the thought to propel myself or others forward. Anything that keeps you from advancement is a chain or a yoke. Regardless to whether you are more comfortable with labeling these things chains or yokes is not the issue. The real issue is that you need to be freed. Chains and yokes can be mentally, physically or spiritually implemented. One thing for certain is that the ability for them to restrain you is based upon your aspect of them. Chains and yokes don't keep you grounded they keep you in slavery. When you are grounded you are free to move about without limitations. When you are chained or yoked, you have a limitation to where you may advance, move or travel. This is why it's important for you to recognize these chains and walk out of them.

Cultural and traditional practices are also forms of chains and yokes. These could present themselves as positives but later render you to negative dispositions. Having the ability and exercising your capabilities to acknowledge these chains will free you while at the same time allow you to practice them without permanent restraints. For those of us that operate in the spiritual realm of Christ, we align these to operating under the law or grace. However you chose to apply these principles or thoughts delved into through your reading of "No More Chains! The Rule 2:22 Principle," you will finish with a new respect for where you presently are in life as to how you approach problems or issues and how you will begin to change the course of your actions and thoughts. Let the journey begin and enjoy this new found wisdom. I anoint each and every one of you right now to take back your life. In Jesus name.

"One of the most antagonistic soirits we fight is self-deception. Self-deception steals from our godly faith and empowers our waivering faith. What are you doing at this exact moment? This will tell you whether you're in control or being led by God."

~Dr. Aqeel Taahir Ash-Shakoor, CDKA~

CHAPTER ONE:

ACKNOWLEDGE

Accept Constructive Criticism

I Corinthians 3:13-17 (King James Holy Bible)

13. Every man's work shall be made manifest: for the day shall declare it, because it shall be revealed by fire; and the fire shall try every man's work of what sort it is. 14. If any man's work abide which he hath built thereupon, he shall receive a reward. 15. If any man's work shall be burned, he shall suffer loss: but he himself shall be saved; yet so as by fire. 16. Know ye not that ye are the temple of God, and that the Spirit of God dwelleth in you? 17. If any man defile the temple of God, him shall God destroy; for the temple of God is holy, which temple ye are.

Constructive criticism builds character. Had anyone told me this, years ago, I would have just understood this to be jealousy. I was used to being criticized for my football accomplishments, which I found generally as a youth to be just plain jealousy. I was used to being criticized because I didn't inform people of my moves through life, which were no more than jealousy of people that I felt weren't changing themselves. I was used to criticism from people who were jealous of things they seen me acquire, such as vehicles that they didn't realized that I had worked so hard for.

Constructive criticism when truthful is one of your best friends. I put a lot into whatever I choose to do. I never claim to be the best, but I do claim to assert myself into whatever I choose full scale. Why would anyone put themselves into something and not be willing to give their all? In order to become a master of your skills, you have to be willing and acceptable to constructive criticism. Constructive criticism will bring out the beast in you. You will accomplish more than you ever would have imagined. Why you may ask? Well, when a person accepts the constructive criticism, they go back to the drawing board and analyze their craft. It's nothing wrong with your raw talent, but in order to conquer certain areas of life, you have to assert your skills or talents with or within certain parameters that are approved or understood by your audience.

Music is one of my favorite examples when it comes to constructive criticism. Most successful singers I'm familiar with grew up generally with a background of singing in church choirs. Now being familiar with church choir singing, singers generally get louder and louder upon the applauding and praising of their audiences. Congregations of high accolades will stand behind anyone of their favorite choir members and tell them they can sing. The truth is that their best choir singer doesn't understand four part harmony nor do they possess the knowledge or skills to sing alto, soprano, and tenor all in one song. Practices generally consist of singing the song harder and louder in the same manner in which they've always sang.

I've seen where these same singers were brought into professional studios and leave disappointed because they made brash statements that everyone was trying to change their singing. Well, if they took the time to understand that music professionals were trying to help them instead of hurting them, they would have understood that they were only striving to perfect their crafts. A lot of people that desire to become professional singers do not realize the amount of time that goes into a hit song or album. Most singers think they can just walk into any studio, at any given time, and record a hit song or album. Your raw talents in church are merely amateur efforts in the professional world of recording. With constructive criticism well received and the assertion of the sharpening tools given in the form of exercises and tips, you would become the next Alicia Keyes, Celine Dion, John Legend, Justin Timberlake, Marvin Sapp, or Tasha Cobbs. Stop, look, and listen! There are people that genuinely wish to help you and not hurt you. Accepting constructive criticism commands and demands certain lines of trust. When you surround yourself with positive people that you honestly do not doubt their existence, then you will be pretty secure in knowing that they have your best interest in mind.

Read business magazines and learn how the professionals have become successful in whatever they chose to do. Their stories are your examples and resources to not make the same mistakes they made through blood, sweat, tears, and most of all, time. Understand that not everyone achieves success in the same manner or at the same time. There are many successful people behind the people whose faces are plastered on posters and television sets. The behind the scene people are the real success stories. They give and have given the successful faces the constructive criticism they needed to become who they are and were. Often times when professionals reach a certain level of success, self admitted, there are ones that lose touch with reality. If they have strong foundations, there are people that snatch them back and let them know the truth. These "keeping it real" people keep us in check of who we are and where we come from. These are your real friends. Real friends are not ones that promote envy and jealousy. Real friends are ones that tell you when your breath smells tart and you need to brush your teeth or eat a mint. Real friends tell you that you have an offensive odor and need to bathe and use a deodorant. Real friends don't sit back and parasite off you, they actually put in work and play their positions without harvesting jealousy of your success, simultaneously ensuring they perform checks and

25

balances of your actions. All of this is pure constructive criticism.

Now, I must be perfectly honest about giving constructive criticism. One must know that constructive criticism should be given in a manner in which the listener or receiver can comprehend the message. The last thing you want to bring about is confrontation as a result of a bruised or scarred ego. I do insist that there are times when constructive criticism must be delivered in raw form. Knowing your audience or receiver and knowing oneself is very important when delivering constructive criticism.

Overall, constructive criticism should be well received, accepted, and demanded of those that claim to have your best interest at hand and in mind. Constructive criticism is like extended family nurturing and support. Pride yourself on the ability to accept constructive criticism, and reward yourself for your ability to take constructive criticism and use it as a profiting tool.

Break the Young Complex
Genesis 1:26-27 (King James Holy Bible)

26. And God said, Let us make man in our image, after our likeness: and let them have dominion over the fish of the sea and over the fowl of the air, and over the cattle, and over all the earth, and over every creeping thing that creepth upon the earth. 27. So God created man in His own image, in the image of God created he him; male and female created he them.

The birth of you is what every father dreamed of. The blessing that was bestowed upon man to have an heir to the throne was soon to be destiny of a king. The power not transferred but shared with your princes and princesses have been misused. The ability to conquer all fears has escaped through unworthiness of knowing and being in touch with the power of one. The one Creator, who blessed the world with a baby boy that would grow into the man that the world patiently awaits his return, was a fleshly man.

In order to know who you are you must understand your birth. Jesus is the past, present, and future. The Gospel of Christ tells us that He was the Word. The Word was with God. As you were in the loins of your father and came forth so was Jesus. Jesus was in the holy of holies with The Father. The Gospel then says that the same was I the beginning with God. You as a young man must understand that physically you are a boy however you as all of us were born with the spirit of God in us. Genesis 1:26-27 details how we were created in the image of God. Once you understand that important point then you should begin to look at yourself in an entirely different light. You were born with an all-knowing spirit. The activation of a man's mind is celebrated when he studies to show himself articulate and intelligent using the knowledge and wisdom that has been imparted upon him at birth. The Gospel of Jesus informs you that you were born with an omni-present spirit. Having an omni-present spirit means you are able to present yourself in any environment as long as you unlock the detrimental downfalls of living in comfort zones. With the Word of God, your presence is able to be felt in multiple places at one time. The essence in which you view yourself is the way that you will live your life and operate throughout the ages.

Likewise, young ladies need to recognize that the same previously mention statements encompass her being. You were created to be man's help meet and not beneath him in any form or fashion in the physical since of God's spiritual order. Yes, man is the head of the household from which you were created. Learn to appreciate the value that God brought you forth in and then you can understand the life He gave you. Man was impregnated with you as you now become impregnated with life to bring forth. Man's ability to bear life was by the surgical hands of God himself. God has now placed this noble and glorious ability in you. Man shares in the process however it is you that carries and brings life forward. You are the mother of civilization.

Ladies your wisdom comes from deep within your godliness to be in obedience to Christ and not man. You submit yourselves as a means to please the Father (God). Your very essence is praise worthy and this prompts man to value his most prize possession. You are not property in the negative sense you are possession of the caretaker. Man is your caretaker as he has been commissioned by God to do just that.

If you were to examine any environment with the presence of young men, you will see them all trying to exercise their dominion over the same territory. We as adults struggle most times with the attempt to calm this God given ability, because we forget and often omit the very essence of who we are as men and what we were created with. We believe that the young boys haven't learned to share when truthfully, they haven't learned to exercise their dominion. They have not learned to exercise their wisdom. This cycle has been perpetuated by those of us that have leaned towards the "I have to have it all mentality."

The surreal but misunderstood nature of these young men is that they really all wish to get along but their guidance has not matured and neither has the adults around them. Adults are the most critical means of nurture for these young men but often they find themselves choosing sides instead of rectifying the urge to subduing everything. Conquering makes a young man and even an adult man feel a sense of accomplishment. Pouting comes through dissatisfaction with our ability to rule. We never wish to finish last because it leads us to believe we have failed. All we know at our young age is that winning is everything. If I can't win, then I don't want to play anymore.

Attitudes of rage can be seen in young men in their very enjoyable moments of individual playing of the favorite PS4 or Xbox games. The young man will be all alone in a challenge to conquer a specific game, but yet the warfare presence sounds like he is playing with approximately three or four other young men. You will hear uncontrollable attitudes, emotional transitions of anger to joy, rages, screams, and yes, profanity. He will lose himself in the ambiance of the façade that has overtaken and catapulting him into the fictional warfare that he has created within his own mind. You can't

32

calm him down because he has accepted the temporary aurora as a surreal moment of time that he honestly feels he is a part of.

Young ladies you are battling with tremendous amounts of self esteem and feeling less empowered than your male counterparts. This becomes dangerous because all you tend to do is fight the care that God has enabled you to receive through your delicateness. You have become chained to the thought that you're not receiving the attention you deserve from poor relationships of a father. You lash out at men because of this very sad matter which your father started. Now, your means is all about taking control and this is a trick of the devil to lure you further from your protective covering.

Young ladies don't know their bodies as they think they do so they give it away freely because of the lack of education. They know of menstrual cycles, pregnancy, and sex but lack the true knowledge of value. This is what propels them into negative arenas of abuse and misuse. They even find themselves battling for position amongst other young ladies with an aggressive and condescending nature. You confuse your negative behaviors with having power which really is a cry-out for more love and affection. This same young lady eventually grows into an adult woman who generally continues the same battle but in an adult body. Your young lady complex continues to control your essence rather than your essence controlling you.

The days of doll babies and tea cup parties with other young ladies are long absent and now you bargain and trade for lavish lifestyles in your adult age that further bury you in the pits of hell. You want to fight back but instead you fight the realness of hurt that has shown you no attention in your own home, your broken family ties, your molestations, your rapes, and your

34

everyday struggles. As much as a true man wishes to help you, he realizes he can't because it's not you he's dealing with, it's the young lady in you that still cries for all that you missed in the past.

In breaking the young man complex, we also find that adult men have failed miserably with the very same learned disposition of dominion. Our disastrous leadership has made us territorial within our homes and warfare has been waged on our families. Our gift of dominion sometimes causes us to place our spouses and children on the enemy's side. There appears to be a need for us to express that we are in charge and wish for everyone to acknowledge our position even in peace time. We become just as touchy as the actual young men and never realize that we are essentially battling within ourselves to break the young man complex.

A true man doesn't have to intrude on the peace of others in order to feel like a man. A true man doesn't have to stand up and tell everyone he's a real man. A true man doesn't have to be abusive in order to feel empowered. A true man is simply a true man because his presence is felt by the displaying of his obedience to God in loving, honoring, respecting, and protecting all that he shall have dominion over. A true man and woman are dependent upon God and not that of themselves. A true man and woman carries not the disposition of the unlearned young complex. A true man and woman has the morals and values of the very essence in which he/she was created. A true man and woman are godly men and women!

Subdue Your Lusts

1 Corinthians 9:27 (King James Holy Bible)

27. But I keep under my body, and bring it into subjection: lest that by any means, when I have preached to others, I myself should be a castaway.

Learn to subdue your lusts at an early age. Learning to subdue the lusts of the heart will institute the act of discipline. Discipline is an ability that all great leaders possess and teach. One, who lives his life disciplined by God, although in the flesh of a man, will have shortcomings, but he will never come up short. He will use his or her shortcomings as steps to elevate their mental and physical beings to the accolades of compelling character.

When you learn to subdue your lusts you are seen in a different light. Women love men that can subdue their lusts and likewise men love women that subdue their lusts. It's no greater damper on relationships than a man that only sees a woman because of the lust in his mind. On the reverse, no man wants to have a woman that lusts after other men. Women also love men that are more in tuned with their creative mind than their sexual mind. Men have greater respect and hold them more

37

worthy of being a wife if they are found as guarding their bodies against lustful and overwhelming promiscuity. Any man or woman can offer sexual thoughts however real men and women with creative and virtuous minds and character are the epitome of a candidate for companionship. Sex is the quick route and shortcoming of invalidating the essence of godliness.

The number of women today that seek sex more than men are overwhelmingly high. If we are to digress for a second, I may add that this point can be substantiated by those same women that profess having been sexually abused, molested, and raped. Yes, this is true. Having counseled and spoken to numerous women of all ages, ethnicities, races, etc. they turned to this life of dominating their partners from the abuse that they suffered. It becomes a phase or lifestyle of domination; more succinctly, being in control. The rage of lust is identified as a thirst for power to assure they stay in control and not be subdued by men. Some of these women find their way into homosexuality nurturing and plotting on the weaknesses of other women having been through the same abuses. It may sound alarming but I find it rather intriguing to hear this from so many women. It's not an area to play the blame game, however we ideally see that it stems from an uncontrollable lust in the pit of hurt. The lust represents a craving to conquer.

Now that your taste buds are savoring for more of that, I'll switch the subject of lust to point out that lust is not all about sex. The lusts of life take on all sorts of identities. Lusts for buying, eating, shopping, spending, etc. are outrageously leading people away from God. I think one of the more noticeable lusts is the shoe fetishes people have. I find it amazing that when new sneakers are soon to be released, the marketing and sales teams strategically tease the lusts of the people.

People camp out day and night outside stores and venues to be the first to own a certain pair of name brand shoes. No, I dare not call the name of the sneakers you already have at the top of your mind because it's not just those sneakers but even certain high class dress shoes with colored bottoms. That explicit inner uncontrolled lust that you not only have to get the newest, first, and only pair, you have to get them in all the various colors.

I wish to present this in the most respectful manner however I believe when you address peoples' lust for food it appears to be a put down. It probably would surprise you more to understand that even skinny people lust for food. The lust for food is saddening because we see obesity overtaking the nation as it has really crippled many of our youth. There's an "eat, eat, eat" mentality and lack of any physical activity. People have become so comfortable with their weight gain and have chosen to satisfy their lust by claiming its an illness. Yes it is an illness and it's called lust. Every other disorder in life is classified as a sickness and the lust for food is no different. We can't control our lusts so we reclassify it to give us more comfort to continue in the same behavior. This becomes the same as a lust for sex. There generally is no lust for exercise here which leads me into the next lust.

The world has become so health conscious at the same time. Even the good things have become a lust in this life. Exercise is a need for the human body but lust and pride of life have conquered a many. Workout fiends have a nasty lust for wanting to workout. Their entire life is wrapped around working out and standing in the mirror admiring their curves and muscles. Now, I will not sit here and act like I don't desire the model body however I'm not sold out to the workout routine. My personal belief is that everyone should have some type of workout regime and stick to it as a means of good health. Our lusts for muscle built bodies create a buying frenzy of multiple weight formulas designed to sculpt the best body. These lust are often found to lead to the use of illegal substances to maintain the results of lustful natures of exercising.

Subduing your lust is not affixed to one area of your life but to every aspect of your life. There are even lusts for people that are not even sexually promoted. We develop all sorts of fixations on celebrities or just our day-to-day persons in society. The word of God warns us against these chains that need breaking however we can't abandon our lusts of the world long enough to develop that kind of obedience to put God's Word into practice. We are a sickly people that don't even realize that we are sick. We are dying from self and continuing to praise the lust that we continue to feed on.

Escape Temptations of the Flesh

I Corinthians 10:13 (King James Holy Bible)

13. There hath no temptation taken you but such as is common to man: but God is faithful, who will not suffer you to be tempted above that ye are able; but will with the temptation also make a way to escape, that ye may be able to bear it.

We, as men, expect that we will not be tested in the flesh. If the very man, Jesus Christ, was tested by Satan and offered the highest gifts of this world, would we not be more than tempted to violate God's law? Temptation lies deep within the inner souls of our bodies. We feel we are strong enough to conquer temptations all by ourselves, without calling on the Lord for assistance.

Have you ever thought what would happen to a NASCAR driver speeding endlessly around a track at top speed, and he would momentarily take his eyes off the cars and roadway ahead of him? It would be very disastrous! Well giving in to temptations of the flesh is much like being on that race track. We are heading down a street at top speed lacking brakes to stop our reckless engagement of the temptations that stop our blessings from Him, who sits Judge Supreme of all.

The very power to prevail in resisting temptation does not rest in being away from that which tempts us. The power to prevail in resisting temptation lies within the Holy Spirit which comforts our souls. How do we encompass that Spirit which gives us comfort to control those uncontrollable urges to give in to temptation? It's really simple…we must invest in the Word of God. We have to breathe, eat, and sleep with the Word as though we physically see the Spirit like that which tempts us. Feed your souls and spirit with that which is righteous and your light will illuminate beacons of rays for all to see. You will be surprised that those situations that tempt you will lose their validity. Their validity lies only within our inability to nurture our souls.

*Let not sin therefore reign in your mortal body, that ye should obey it in the lusts thereof. Neither yield ye your instruments of unrighteousness unto sin: but yield yourselves to God, as those that are alive from the dead, and your members as instruments of righteousness unto God. For sin shall not have dominion over you: for ye are not under that law, but under grace **(Romans 5:12-14 King James Holy Bible).***

Let not sin therefore rule as king in your mortal (short-lived, perishable) bodies, to make you yield to its cravings and be subject to its lusts and evil passions. Do not continue offering or yielding your bodily members [and faculties] to sin as instruments (tools) of wickedness. But offer and yield yourselves to God as

45

though you have been raised from the dead to
[perpetual] life, and your bodily members [and
faculties] to God, presenting them as implements of
righteousness. For sin shall not [any longer] exert
dominion over you, since now you are not under Law
[as slaves], but under grace [as subjects of God's favor
and mercy] **(Romans 5:12-14 Amplified/ Parallel**
Meaning King James Holy Bible).

Let us be mindful in that "a thought leads to a desire,
a desire leads to an addiction, an addiction leads to an
affliction, and an affliction leads to a conviction!"

We put ourselves in predicaments that we know are
harmful to our souls and spirits. We feel too
embarrassed to tell unrighteous boys and men that we
do not feed off the filth that they marvel.

As discussed earlier on, Leaders act off what they
know is correct and not off what others think they
should. Would you gamble your salvation on being

able to talk amongst the crowds and receive applauds, which die down by nightfall, in exchange for an eternal place with the Lord, free from all troubles and worries? If you hesitate the least answering that, then your salvation is already in jeopardy! Crave the Lord and that which compliments your souls, for we have been promised victory.

"Stop holding people accountable for that which you were responsible for protecting, and stop, making people responsible for that which you will not be held accountable for!"

~Dr. Aqeel Taahir Ash-Shakoor, CDKA~

CHAPTER TWO:

CONFESS

Receive Salvation (Testimony)

Psalms 23: 4-5 (King James Holy Bible)

4. Yea, though I walk through the valley of the shadow of death, I will fear no evil: for thou art with me; thou rod and thy staff they comfort me. 5. Thou preparest a table before me in the presence of mine enemies: thou anointest my head with oil; my cup runneth over.

Leaders perform their duties with courage and strength. One that embraces these enchanting and revered verses of strength cannot deny that the Word of God is alive and dwells in them. The leader will have an abundance of certainty and uplift to drive forward knowing that all his needs will not only be addressed, but fulfilled. I cannot express the assurance of power that I felt as I rededicated my life to Christ. I prayed for years that God would eventually reveal to me the true message that he wanted me to go forth and minister. Did this mean that I immediately became a minister, No! Ministering the Word was a part of my daily actions even when I professed Islam. On December 27, 2009, I entered church for regular service just enjoying a continued weekend of family time endured by my family. That Thursday, December 25, 2009, I received my final confirmation that God delivered to me. All I can describe to you is that when I began to pray and ask God to give me a clear confirmation of his will to be done, I broke. I broke down in a godly manner, as tears of joy and relief filled my eyes and heart. I had finally been spoken to through his infinite wisdom. I did not hear a voice audibly! I did not see any fictitious beings! I was not taken up through the clouds! I stood as a normal or mortal man in my secret closet (a clean quiet place sanctified to God) in my home and was moved by God being inspired by the Spirit to go forth and preach his word. So that Sunday morning, just before entering into the inner doors of the church, I told my mother I was going to rejoin the church. She then asked if I wanted to meet the minister. I agreed. Upon meeting the minister, he asked me if I was really ready and have accepted the Lord Jesus Christ as my Saviour, and believed that he died on the cross for our sins. I immediately answered, "Yes sir!" He then said, "Okay my brother, I will address this in the Invitation to Christ part of the service." When that time came, the minister began to explain how and what it was to receive the invitation to Christ. As the minister continued on with his explanation, I pressed my mother's leg, nudged my wife, and walked towards the Alter. How real could this be that in this very same church, in front of this very same pulpit, many years ago around the age of 9 or 10, I was baptized and became a member of the church! I rededicated my life proclaiming Jesus Christ as my

Lord and Saviour and gave testimony that I did not leave God or Jesus when I converted to Islam; I simply left the ways of the people. I explained through joyful tears and shattered words that I had been moved to rejoin the church and answer my calling to preach God's Word, as my grandmother had firmly stated to me as a youth. Her firm statement was that I was going to be a Preacher and Professor one day. How fitting could this be that in the year of 2010, I completed my Masters of Science Degree in Criminal Justice and began instructing college classes as an Adjunct Professor with Roanoke Chowan Community College, Ahoskie, N.C., while serving on the Technology Advisory Board for Criminal Justice, all while God called me to preach the Gospel of Christ.

Hear my cry, O God; attend unto my prayer. From the end of the earth will I cry unto thee, when my heart is overwhelmed; lead me to the rock that is higher than

I. For thou hast been a shelter for me, and a strong tower from the enemy. I will abide in thy tabernacle for ever: I will trust in the covert of thy wings. Selah. For thou, O God, hast heard my vows: thou hast given me the heritage of those that fear thy name (Psalms 61: 1-5).

For all that I can tell you, anyone who has known me during my 20 year stint in Islam, I walked in peace, prayed continuously, and strived to get closer to God, and strived in building a godly relationship. Acknowledging my Saviour once more, has now dressed me back in the King's garments and placed the crown of His reward back upon my head. Here I stand a Leader honoring God's power and witnessing Jesus Christ has provided the instructional manual on how to receive salvation.

Stop Fighting and Let the Lord

Exodus 14:14 (King James Holy Bible)

14. The Lord shall fight for you, and you shall stand your peace.

Any great leader should know how to fight without throwing a punch. It took me some time to learn this concept that I have developed. Truly trial and error of acting out physically and verbally were not the best way for me to be victorious in my battles. I had to reason with myself and understand that *power energized is power exercised.*

I remember back in 1990, at Marine Corps Air Base MWSS 272, New River, N.C., I was just a Lance Corporal. Well during this time I was filling a Sergeant's billet in the tactical motor pool. I was in charge of Marines for the Medium section of vehicles which were 5-ton vehicles. My sergeant, who I had not met, was in Honduras as I, myself, had just completed a two-month term on air contingency. Quickly, I learned my section's responsibility as well as the location and/or vehicle discrepancy and echelon of maintenance. I worked diligently to build my team full of Lance Corporals on down to privates. We became a tight knit team with in the motor pool. We ate together, we lived together, we partied together, we played together, and we worked together. I projected myself upon them and taught them my "mirror concept." My "mirror concept" is that when people see me, they see them. I was always sharp in my uniform from head to toe. Just because we worked in grease daily, I didn't accept my Marines coming into morning formations with yesterday's grease under their nails or on their uniforms.

Now of course, I immediately caught the eye of my peers and superiors, such as Corporals on up to the

Officer-in-Charge, which was a Second Lieutenant. I sparked jealousy from Corporals of the small and heavy sections, which were always wrinkled and mangy in their uniforms. Surprisingly through time and just not settling for learning my job, I learned the jobs of each section head and the maintenance echelon of all their vehicles. It wasn't long after, that I could quote the number of every vehicle in the motor pool, which section it belonged to, what echelon of maintenance it was in, and if it was serviceable.

Well, one particular day when my section and I were driving Marines back from the rifle range, when I reached the motor pool, my friend and coworker, came up to me angry, as if he was ready to fight. Of course, I picked up on it immediately and asked what was wrong. He told me that one of the Corporals from the other sections told him he had to work late in the motor pool, while he let his people go home early. I need to remind you that all the work for our section was completed for that day, as it was prior to quitting time daily. I anxiously told him that's not going to fly! I hurried and parked the 5-ton I was driving and found the Corporal, who issued the order. When I found him, I told him, "Look! We've been on the road since 0330 (3:30 a.m.), while everyone else was in the rack and you think you are going to keep my Marines back, while you let your Marines go home early. I continued by saying, I don't care what anybody says, he is not going to work late." I have to admit that I was far over my pay grade to speak to a Corporal like that, but I never been the one to not stand up for what is right. That's what great leaders do, correct? Anyway, I was ordered to report to the Master Gunnery Sergeant of the motor pool. When I reported, I immediately began to rattle off with my frustration. Before I could get half way into my statement, Master Gunnery Sergeant told me to lock my body up, which meant to come to the position of attention. He asked me why was a Lance Corporal chewing (scolding) out his Corporals? When I finally had the chance to speak, I started by telling Master Gunnery Sergeant that if rank is going to make it right, then it's no reason for me to speak. He told me to proceed. After telling Master Gunnery Sergeant what had taken place and then adding the point that no one in the motor pool besides me, not even him, could quote the numbers and status of every vehicle in the motor pool. I told him that our section is far above ready daily than any section, and we are the sharpest section in the motor pool. Well shortly thereafter, the Master Gunnery Sergeant told me to get out of his office and tell those Corporals to report to him. I already knew the walls were going to come down. As soon as the door shut, Master Gunnery Sergeant commenced to give them a good old fashion Marine Corps chewing out. Now, right after the

Corporals left the office, Master Gunnery Sergeant called for me once again. I have to admit that at this time, I was asking myself, why would he need to see me again? When I marched into the office and centered myself on Master Gunnery Sergeant's desk, he paused, just before telling me to report to company formation early Monday morning, because I was being promoted to Corporal. He smirked and then told me to get out of his office.

This is how I, as a leader, fought without throwing a punch. I commanded and not demanded anything but the best from my team and myself. Our appearance was always immaculate, while our camaraderie was impeccable. We exercised the true meaning of teamwork and being a team player. When they saw my Marines, they saw me. We were sharp in our knowledge and we took pride in our uniforms and vehicles. We added our own personal touches to our vehicles within Marine Corps regulation. Just from doing what was expected of us and going beyond the means to stay sharp is how we commanded the attention and praise that we deserved.

The Corporals were no match for my uncanny leadership ability to influence others, as it was beyond my knowing at the time. I was winning a fight that I never landed a physical punch. Yes! By all means we were ready to go fist-to-cuff, but that would have demeaned our whole character. We knew we had everyone beat and we even tried to show other Marines our effectiveness, but jealous noncommissioned officers stood in our way.

Subsequently, upon my promotion to Corporal, I was also appointed the inspection noncommissioned officer for the motor pool. Those Corporals that once supervised me and hated my existence feared retaliation. I honestly wanted to retaliate now that I had the chance, but I did it according to Marine Corps regulation and let's just say that after I held my first official inspection of them, I didn't have to worry about them anymore. I earned my respect, as well as the understanding that I was willing to help them instead of hurting them. We all became much closer, as they now came to me for guidance.

As long as you do what is expected of you, those that harass you will soon be T-K-Oed! You don't have to wish bad things on them or pray for their downfall, you just have to work diligently and pray for your success. You will win convincingly, without ever having to throw a single punch! If we could just remember that success is championed by God. All of our battles are already won if we would only approach them with the true faith of God. Sometimes matters may seem very intimidating however that intimidation is really fear projected because the principalities observe the natural spirit of God's presence within you. You don't have to do anything but that which God has commanded us to do. We just have to trust God! We just have to preach the Gospel in season and out of season not being shame of our savior. That is the true victory of any battle we could ever face. Don't focus on get-back or revenge just focus on serving God and watch all your troubles fall by the way side.

"The devil has no compassion for heart. He tinkers with your life and just as you think you're over him you realize that you are still who you thought you left behind. Your thoughts are confusing as you battle between the devil and discernment. The real choice in this matter is whether you will really trust God to expose it or continue to run from it. God really wants for you to be free in Him alone."

~Dr. Aqeel Taahir Ash-Shakoor, CDKA~

CHAPTER THREE:

REBUKE

Poison Interference

I Corinthians 10:4-5 (King James Holy Bible)

4. And did all drink the same principal drink: for they drank of that spiritual Rock that followed them: and that Rock was Christ. 5. But with many of them God was not well pleased: for they were overthrown in the wilderness.

Jesus Christ desires for us all to be healthy in what we consume. The indication here is that the disciples all drank the same drink as He did. There was no deviation or separation of what was offered for drink. The water that was received from the rock was real water. Being that this water was given at the divine intervention of God, it took on a spiritual symbolism. In short, the water and rock that we should affix ourselves to is Christ. The spiritual Rock and Christ is what was partaken, followed, and remained with them.

At times in life, you will be required to quench your thirst for knowledge desired and information destined to be received. How will you accept that which comes to you? Will you drink from a nutritious fountain or from one which comes in bountiful amounts, but is so polluted it decays the very substance of your inner stability? The true answer is that most of us will choose to drink the poison supplied by those that are in no way profitable to our well-being. These are the very ones we have befriended through acquaintances and they smile and offer derogatory remarks that curve our viewing of others.

This is often seen in many people that profess Christianity and have been incarcerated and found themselves studying various religions or even a normal person in society seeking truth. The poison penetrates their minds because in the manner in which they have collectively gathered all this knowledge together but cannot decipher what is true anymore. The poison will have them believe that the entire reason they went searching would be because Christianity doesn't work. Well let me set this up now so we can really see the poison as it processes. First, Christianity is not viewed as working or not working because it is Christ that we are in that has already done a great work. The entire world and world of religions are awaiting the return or Christ and they all give their reason for the wait. One thing we cannot escape is that Christ will return, so it's better that we're already following Christ than being sorry we missed the boat when He returns.

Second, the poison is mixed with slight truths, wrong. Poison can never mix with truth however it can tangle itself alongside truth and this is what causes the people to become entangled in the doubting web. Christianity or Christ needs no lawyer to fight for it. The Gospel itself is here for reproof, correction and instruction in righteousness that the man of God will be thoroughly furnished unto all good works. Now, there is no way to poison this fountain unless you remove yourself and begin to sip something not coming from the fountain of Christ. Sounding good and tasting good is not an accreditation for the passing score of God. This is the recipe for disaster.

Working with Dell and Hewlett Packard are totally different. They all speak the computer language but no employee of Dell can go to a Hewlett Packard training and comeback and work in the knowledge of Dell's company and believe they are following the guidelines. Just because things seem familiar do not make them familiar. This is why we have to ensure we know the mission and vision statements of the companies we work for. Not knowing the mission and vision statements will cause employees to adlib their work experiences and skills. The company has to be on one accord. Hewlett Packard is poison to Dell as Dell is poison to Hewlett Packard.

Picture a classroom setting where the instructor or teacher is asking students to introduce themselves. As the class consecutively follows through giving their brief biographies and experiences, there will be those that snarl and frown making faces to entice others to show no appreciation or give respect to the presenter. This person or persons will continue to make undesirable remarks as those that are more knowledgeable and experienced than he or she is in order to discredit the presenter. You may initially buy into the motivation that is supplied through attentive listening of other presenters, but the overwhelming human flaw of accepting negative connotations pours endlessly through our milking minds.

The undeniable truth is that you have begun to drink the poison supplied by those who seek to kill our ambitions and carve out an essential part of our souls. These blood suckers and parasites live merely to eat the flesh of those that tend to feed our highest proverbial appetites for success. Nothing is more mentally disastrous to one's mental growth than poison filtered through channels or environments of learning. What we intake is what we output. Our minds are digestive systems. Bad information and insulting comments are poison to the flesh and makeup of healthy minds and productive thoughts. Poison or negative information is highly desired because the taste and fulfillment tends to be greater on the individual's mind than the awareness of health and longevity. Like the human body, the tongue tells the body that the poison tastes good when it's mixed to the taster's approval, but the conscious mind tells the body that no matter how well the poison is prepared or appears to be, it deteriorates the fleshly body as does the poisonous thoughts eat away at the

71

productive brain. One step backwards tends to be greater than two steps forward. The negative outweighs the good in human perception. One can do a lifetime of good and one bad incident can steal the character and/or thunder right from under you. The age old battle of good versus evil is a reality.

What will you do in the face or deceit? Will you succumb to the pervasive poison or will you filter the tainted images and feed off the integrity of the message and messenger? All of us are tested daily and clues of poisonous intervention displayed like bleached spots on colored laundry. As long as you take heed to the following message, you will forever filter subtle poison. "Separate the weak from the obsolete and retreat from those that speak behind clinched teeth."

Don't Freeload on Others' Liberties

Ecclesiastes 2:24 (King James Holy Bible)

24. There is nothing better for a man, than that he should eat and drink, and that he should make his soul enjoy good in his labor. This also I saw, that it was from the hand of God.

No one would ever want to believe they are a freeloader. Most attitudes that we present cause us to insert our character in the freeloading zone. Freeloading presents itself as compromising for the betterment of a relationship. However, the reality of freeloading is the selfish nature of those that wish to remain the same while inadvertently manipulating matters to tip the scales in our favor.

Our experiences contain variables that are triggered through association of identical means by which we have learned to cope in order to bring us peace. The informal structuring of these newly found guidelines or rules that have ushered us into our present lives has become our comfort zone of operation. Anyone or anything that opposes or attempts to bring about changes to our ideals becomes the enemy. Unbeknownst to the unwilling flesh, we perceive our ideals to be the soul truth and nothing but the truth and we will do anything to bolster our methods upon others' liberties.

In the civilian world, one would consider these actions second degree trespassing. Second degree trespassing on others' liberties is established when one attempts to embark upon others' freedoms, morale, and welfare in the life cycle. Once others' oppose your embarking, any continued actions of this nature critically changes the charges to first degree trespassing. Freeloading commences the very second friendships or relationships are established and you do not incur any cost or lost for your unchanging behaviors.

The "this is my seat in church mentality" comes to mind here. People in general that attend church will repetitiously commit to patterned behaviors such as sitting on the same pew and in the same place on the pew Sunday after Sunday. Time indirectly tells the person that because they arrive at church each Sunday and that particular seat is open, it should be understood that this is their seat. Pews are not posted with reserved signs however the certain pew has become their comfort zone for attending church service. If we were to arrive to service late on any given Sunday and find someone sitting in the very same place that we have sat for an extended period of time, we would expect for others to conform to our comfort zone principles. This would upset our psyche so much that we would insist that others put aside their liberties in order to understand that this has been the means by which we have operated successfully. The courtesy of others' to set aside their liberties and move over for us opens the door to us becoming a freeloader. You are insisting that you have it all together and freeload on others' liberties of their positive attitudes to work with you in your selfish world.

Trying to change others is not the answer to our problems. Our problems are the mere factor of us not wanting to accept that we stumbled into the freeloader characterization through seeking comfort. Changes have nothing to do with others' attitudes or behaviors. Changes have everything to do with our choice of liberties. Choosing to exercise the correct liberty removes the freeloading banner from our persons and establishes a communication breakthrough that is ideally unspoken (by audible means). Pay your fines for freeloading and set yourself free!

Be careful not to become an uninformed freeloader. An uninformed freeloader is one that is given up something valuable in order to enjoy the liberties of others' comfort or lifestyles. The uninformed freeloader may appear to be in charge however they are really dependent upon others for companionship, finances, friendships, material recognition, and relationships. The uninformed freeloader can appear altogether however they are a body of confusion. The uninformed freeloader is one that bears deep hurt and the way they are coping with their freeloading is to abuse the liberties of others. The uninformed freeloader will deny they are intruding on others' liberties because they lack the assurance of breaking free from the source of dependency to really feel the independent world.

The independent world forces the uninformed freeloader to face the realness of who they have become. The very person or persons you are freeloading on become the victim of your abusive behavior and truthfully they only continue to allow you to abuse them because they too bear some dependency upon having you freeload. That's it! Yes, in like manner the person that has become the victim is also the perpetrator as they are also freeloading on your liberties. You both will continue to lose out on the true liberties God has intended for us to have. The pursuit of freedom and bountiful living through Jesus is the glorious life.

Avoid Unprofitable Matters

Titus 3:9 (King James Holy Bible)

9. But avoid foolish questions, and genealogies, and contentions, and strivings about the law; for they are unprofitable and vain.

I struggled with this earlier on in life and I can also say for a fair part of my adult life. I made it my duty to do what ever I could to battle against people with negative connotations. If they spoke ill of religious matters, I fought them to the end. If they spoke ill of racial matters, I fought them to the end. If they spoke ill of women, I fought them to the end. If they spoke with a lack of business sense in an egotistical manner, I fought them to the end. At the end of the day, you know what I accomplished! I accomplished ABSOLUTELY NOTHING!

Most of the time when you engage in conversations with people that are less educated on a particular topic, you are generally entering into less than intellectual conversation. Not referring to people being dumb or stupid, you will find that a lot of unfocused people lacking knowledge of current events simply talk just to be talking. When this happens, you generally can expect that your conversing will be derogatory and unprofitable. For instance, I like the way Sports Center advertised one or two of their commercials. In order to be in a solid sports conversation, they cited people as viewing the latest Sports Center news and updates so they could control a sports conversation the next day at work.

Don't waste your positive energy on people that argue just for the sake of arguing. Real leaders don't waste valuable brain power on negative matters. Negative matters come in the form of drawn out telephone conversations that are repetitive and uninformative, as it relates to your leadership statue. Negative matters come in the form of evil or down trodden remarks which attack your goals.

One of the first things you should ask yourself about the conversation that someone else or you are initiating is what is the aim of the conversation? This is like English 101. What is the subject of the conversation? Is the conversation progressing? Is the conversation about the two parties involved or concerning a third party? Third party conversations occurring without the subject of the conversation generally end up being matters of negativity. I can't remember too many conversations that someone has come to me about a third party that ended up being positive. When people seek to inquire about others, I generally ask them have they spoken to the person. Of course that person always makes an excuse for not having addressed the third party.

Positive leaders will not let people bring toxic waste into the intelligent kitchen. See, in the intelligent kitchen of a leader there's always a progressive thought being cooked up. If that leader allows toxic waste to be poured into there kitchen then no one will desire to eat from their kitchen when they serve knowledge or at this point...gossip.

Negative matters come in the form of the company you keep, which are not beneficial in your personal or business lives. Negative matters come in the form of occupying quality time with hours watching comedy, videos, and sports. Television and music are great past time relaxation means, but they are also leading distracters of higher education. Think about it! When is the last time you read an informative book about business building or self-improvement for relaxation? If you have to think about it for even a second, then it's just too long. Whether you are seeking to be the next

Bill Gates, Oprah Winfrey, Christy Walton, Steve Jobs, Bob Johnson, or President Barack Obama, rest assured that you will not secure that status partying and indulging in activities that do not feed the business leader's mind. Understand that none of these greats arrived at their current statuses, however you assumed they started, by sitting around drinking, smoking, and hitting every club and concert with the masses. Looks are deceiving! As most of us see them enjoying the fruits of their labor, there were and are tremendous amounts of leadership building skills they had to hone and continuously practice. Leadership is not free! True leaders earn leadership through blood, sweat, and tears. Yes! They work for it! And they work on it! They acquire the appropriate knowledge and spend time dwelling in the knowledge.

The next time you find yourself engaged in a conversation, monitor your watch and time the actual parts of the conversation that were beneficial to your growth. You will be amazed at your findings. Run with this thought if you will. If you hang around nine scavengers, then you will become the tenth one! If you hang around and learn amongst nine positive and successful persons, you will be the tenth one! The reason is that your brain and creative thoughts are growing upon what you feed it. This is even seen within the prison population. Many argue that prison does not rehabilitate, but educates criminals to become better or more deviant criminals. When a shoplifter goes to jail or prison, he becomes enabled with the skills of murderers, child molesters, bank robbers, rapist, etc. He begins to adapt to his environment. Consciously and subconsciously, he or she learns from patterned behaviors of others that are not positively influencing his or her rehabilitation. Hakeem Olajuwon didn't get to be one of the greatest centers to ever play the game of basketball by perfecting his skills running in the streets with delinquents, dropouts, and drug dealers. Leaders perfect their skills amongst those with skills.

Mind Your Business

1 Thessalonians 4:11-12 (King James Holy Bible)

11. and that ye study to be quiet, and to do your own business, and to work with your own hands, as we commanded you; 12. That ye may walk honestly toward them that are without, and that ye may have lack of nothing.

Let others witness your works of God by living a quiet life putting your hands to work in Kingdom building and not Kingdom destruction. Focus on your service. Are you invested in Kingdom building? If not, why not? Find your place and exercise your gifts and talents. Keep the focus God-centered. Keep away from distractions of what others are doing and look up only to praise God. Concentrate, meditate, and pray more often.

When we desire to know why we are longsuffering in ailments, diseases, finances, low self-esteem, sicknesses, sorrows, etc. All we have to do is look at our own business. Some of us are so busy trying to mind someone else's business in public and secrecy like we have our lives altogether. We need to take our hands and mouths off of each other and put our hands to work for God. If you are participating in the ongoing perversion of listening to those who pervert your ears with foolishness you are not minding your business and the fruits of your labor are sin.

It's very easy to identify unfruitful people who claim Jesus as their Savior. They are the ones that come to you and begin by saying, "Let me ask you something or let me tell you something about so and so; Hey did you know so and so did such and such; Well if it was me I would have done this and that; That don't make sense about this and that and they've done or are doing the same thing." These people are always in the middle of drama or spreading it.

The fact about it all is that they cannot show you any positive fruits of the Kingdom of God but their baskets are full of fruits of backbiting, blame, envy, evil, jealousy, self-betrayal, self-deception, selfishness, etc. They are the same convicted by this scripture and grumbling in the spirit when the truth has been a double-edged sword. Opportunist on a negative adventure will always leach upon the lives of the productive servants.

It doesn't take as much as you may think to fall out the race. Once you glance over at the next runner you have fell behind. The winner is always the one that doesn't look back or have to look to the side. The real winner knows that the only thing in front of him is the finish line and the only things behind him are things that don't have any effect on what lies before him.

The life we live is like graphing paper. In each set you get a pair of numbers that have to take you from one point to the next. The only way a straight line can be drawn between the points is that after we set our initial point then we have to scale the lines to set on our next point in order to draw a straight line. A straight line is the shortest distance between two points. The two points are you and God. God has planted you and he is omnipresent. The shortest distance is the straight and narrow. Advancement in the Kingdom cannot be accomplished by plotting negative attitudes or demeanors. In this imperfect world, we battle with Satan daily as his business is our business. Satan desires not to mind his own affairs but to take every chance at minding our business.

Minding the affairs of others is intrusive and misdirecting your own progress as God has plans for you that are designed just for you. Should you continue an endless journey of people watching and investing in others' business, your life will reflect that of turmoil sooner or later. The devil lives wherever we invite him into. The devil will whisper into your ear-gates the secrets of sin and make it so appealing to you that you'll be well on your way with evil-speaking, blasphemy, whispering and murmuring before you realize what has happened.

We also need to ensure that we train up our children in like manner. Children are soaking up these traits right amongst their parents. Children hear you talking about so and so and in the most awkward times they will call you out on it? We must teach them to be their brother's keeper, by bearing one another's burdens and sorrows. Children should not be involved in our evil-speaking, nor should we. This is a foundation being built for hate and Jesus stated that hating is murder.

If we plan to mind someone else's business then we should be ready and available to help them and not cause more hurt. Anyone that maneuvers around to destroy the reputation of others is a murderous-slandering soul. You cannot speak godly from the same mouth you slander others with. We must keep ourselves out of others' business affairs and render aid when needed through the wisdom provided in the Gospel of Christ.

"Don't make apologies based on it just being the right thing to do, base the right thing to do on the ideas which will not need apologies. Don't confuse your past with your present. Set your soul and spirit free from attachments you know are unhealthy. Some would say practice what you preach however if what you preach is distorted then so will be your practice."

~Dr. Aqeel Taahir Ash-Shakoor, CDKA~

CHAPTER FOUR:

BELIEVE

Build Order and Destroy Chaos

Ecclesiastes 3:1-3 (King James Holy Bible)

1. TO EVERY thing there is a season, and a time to every purpose under the heaven: 2. A time to be born, and a time to die; a time to plant, and a time to pluck up that which is planted; 3. A time to kill, and a time to heal, a time to break down, and a time to build up;

Building and destroying is a lucrative means of leadership. You must first be enthused with creating order for effective and positive gains. Once you are enthused about initiating this just cause, you will quickly move to destroy any chaos that stands in your way.

I put back on my Drill Instructor cover (hat) for this phase of leadership. As I was employed as a Correctional Officer/Drill Instructor at Southampton

Intensive Treatment Center (Bootcamp), I would fiend for my workdays. I would be at home awaiting my return to work and filled with anxiety to train. I love order, as it has been my way of life, since a young man. Most people that know me think that my order came from the Marine Corps alone. This is incorrect, but I will voluntarily admit that the Marine Corps reinforced all order that was instilled in me and instilled that which I lacked.

I loved working the early shift which started at 0500 in the morning. I and one other Drill Instructor were charged with the duty of conducting morning physical training (PT). We would arrive to work prior to 0500 and upon our arrival, we would review our work schedules. Promptly at 0500, we would pop the gates to the living quarters and come through barking orders, as the probationers quickly came to a position of attention standing on line at the center of the squad bay.

You can just imagine how hard it is to be awakened in the morning, by highly motivated, truly dedicated, and wide-awake individuals, who enjoyed training. The probationers came to attention and commenced counting off in a uniform count procedure. Following through with being turned to make up their racks and get dressed for physical training. The day was well on its way. Here stood approximately 30 to 40 individuals, who chose to go against the grain in violating the law. Their lives were totally about selling drugs, using drugs, and any nonviolent crime as a first time felon, and it was strictly a volunteer program. Did they really want order in their lives or were they simply trying to escape the years of incarceration that were suspended by the ruling judge? Well, either way they were here now. These probationers were chaotic when they first arrived at the Bootcamp. They cried, they refused, they slacked, they moaned, they groaned, and they tried to

95

finagle the system. Needless to say, none of that worked. The Bootcamp Program was set up in simulation to the Marine Corps style of training and the Drill Instructors were certified by Marine Corps standards.

Refreshingly, I stood proud to be part of an organization that was put in place to bring order to troubled individual's lives. There were periods of instructions given to demonstrate how chaotic these probationers' lives were and what it would take to organize them in every aspect of their lives. As with any good system of organization, there are always those that believe they are smarter than the system or they can beat the system. So they had to go! When you are not organized and refuse to follow the rules of the game, you lose. For anyone who believes they can win by breaking the rules of the game, just ask the many incarcerated individuals that are and were locked behind the bars of any jail, penitentiary, or prison.

Once the probationers progressed through the 3 month program, they began to follow orders with less penalties and punishments. Waking up in the morning at 0500 and physical training became a reward and not a punishment. They began to understand that bringing organization to their lives made things much easier. They also began to understand that those who continued to rebel were detrimental to their team. Teamwork was seen as family functioning to complete a mission. They felt whole again. They felt like they could take on the world once again. They began to learn to work for no pay which was later found that they committed themselves to work to learn special trades and crafts that they never imagined doing. Drug dealing could not compare to the life changing that the order in their lives gave them.

Graduation day was filled with excitement and harvesting of scared feelings. They were about to be turned loose and back into the world from which they came. Would they succeed or would they fail? Well, for the most part during the time I was employed, the graduates were very successful and very few returned to crime. There were some that got locked up the same night they graduated. You see, they still learned an important lesson that night. You can fake your way through any organized event, but you cannot fake yourself out. When you think you are cheating the system, you are only cheating yourself. Now they have to serve those 20, 30, to 40 years that was suspended, while they now wish they had honestly took in the lessons of order and building their organizational skills. They had three months to plan, do right and be successful. Some chose to return to their unorganized lives of crime. So, now they live under the order of the prison system by the ruling and order of other men and women.

Traffic lights command order. Picture yourself at a busy city intersection with no stoplights. Who has the right-of-way? Who will respect the right-of-way? Who will plow through the intersection without stopping? Who will even go near the intersection? This is a very detailed matter in which chaos can interrupt order. The challenge for you as a leader is to respect order and submit to follow through with order. There can only be one head, for there will be chaos as how the body will be guided. Any conflict in order will result in chaos and a failed mission. Anyway you choose to slice the pie, just remember you have to pick up the cutter first. That's order! You can't slice the pie, if you don't first pick up the cutter. You follow a line of order to successfully achieve the efforts of destroying chaos. Chaotic events occur only as a result of those persons, who violate the sequence of events that are not beneficial for the existence order. So as we started, we also end with *"TO EVERY thing there is a season, and a time to every purpose under the heaven."*

Think Beyond the Bars and Walls
St. John 8:31-32 (King James Holy Bible)

31. Then said Jesus to those Jews which believed on him, If ye continue in my word, then are ye my disciples indeed; 32. And ye shall know the truth, and the truth shall make you free.

One thing that I have noticed and paid close attention to in my years of working in the Department of Corrections is that most offenders walk around like they are still on the streets. I used to walk around and just think "Why in the world do they think they are so hard, just because they have been in prison for years?"

Brothers and sisters in the various prisons are still in slavery. You are not free in mind, because you still harbor feelings of the streets. Every day I heard different brothers and sisters opposing peace in order to be conniving and deceitful.

As much I have walked around speaking in their favor telling officers that they are still humans, I couldn't understand why the offenders were so bitter. Why would you be bidder, because you committed a crime and was punished by the system? We can go around and around about who's innocent and who's guilty, but whoever confesses to sincere guilt has taken the largest step in their life towards freeing themselves from the physical prison. Mentally, you do more harm to yourselves being mad at everybody from the outside to the inside that you come into contact with daily. The offenders around you planning and plotting evil events and conjuring up evil thoughts are not your friends.

They are the actual people who help keep you locked in slavery. It is one thing to say you are free in mind, but when you conduct yourself like you're locked up, then you're actually locked up.

Officers do just as much time behind bars as prisoners do. They pull time with you brothers and sisters. They spend most of their lives behind bars, just to support their families. Now let me take a moment to clear the air. I speak to those that are guilty of the above mentioned acts, because I know that not all officers conduct themselves professionally. I have had many offenders treat me one way and then come back later when they are by themselves and apologize. They give me excuses like, "Man, I thought you were like so and so officers! Officers always treating us like we're not human! You'll ain't trying to help nobody!" My first statement to them is, "Did I treat you like that or did you treat me like you thought I would respond based on other officers' actions?" They generally confess that they were wrong for assuming the evil thoughts first. I then begin to tell them that we, the officers, are or were one mistake away from being in jail. We, the officers have stolen, smoked marijuana, driven while drunk, beat on women, and believe it or not, some have even committed murders. Sounds crazy right? Well it's not! We have officers that are taking their families for a ride as well as the people that work with them on a day-to-day basis, because these people are actually trying to be gang affiliated or trying to show people they are a thug or at the least a street savvy person. Now, the real killers can spot these fake, wanna-be officers a mile away. They are not your friends and nor are they of any positive benefit to your situation. Don't think for a minute that they won't write you up and have you on lockdown.

What is your ultimate goal? Are you striving to be free or are you striving to correct and improve yourselves? If your priority is just striving to be free again, then your priority is all wrong. Striving to correct and improve self should be your aim in life through a relationship with Christ. We have this complacent spirit within us that seeks to keep us right where we are. When we accept Christ and allow the Holy Spirit to move within us freely, the evil spirits have no choice but to leave us. You just need to concentrate on being in the right, every second of the day. If you spend more time character building, I promise you that you will not have the time to get caught up into that which will continue to keep you incarcerated in the mind.

What you're doing is hiding behind the guilt of your past. You don't know how to say I'm sorry without looking like you're weak and feeling like a punk, as they say in prison. Let me tell you this, if you do not accept this role, you will punk down (as the street lingo goes) to those that want you to stay incarcerated like them. Once you admit to yourself and confess to God that you are guilty, it is then that you will be able to see that Christ has been with you the entire time. He just wanted you to change the condition of yourselves, so that you could clearly see the prosperous path that has been lying before you.

The more you focus on Him the more you will see the gates of righteousness open before you. Please know that you are only in prison because anyone that violates law must be punished, but you have been forgiven by Him. No one walks unpunished, no matter how you see it. Punishment doesn't always come right away. It may be years down the road when you go through something that you may not even realize why it's happening. Just smile and say Lord I accept your will and I humbly obey, that I may make peace with you, myself, and others. Don't confuse that thought with trying to please people, because there are some people that no matter what you do in this life, they will never be forgiving or pleased.

One area that you can greatly affect is directing these young brothers and sisters that are going through all links to become prison affiliated. They think prison is a social club that gives them some type of credit with the streets. They feel they will be highly accepted in life if they just get behind bars for a short stay. Some of these young men and women are trying to launch their Rap careers, so they feel they have to have a story. I wonder at times are they aware that some have died seeking this lifestyle. I wonder have they ever listened to "GangStar", when Guru rapped about "Just to Get a Rep!" Some of you are so caught up on these young artists and seeking to be another god. I've been listening to Hip Hop all my life and I still have an ear for the positive messages.

What will be your guidance in directing these newly incarcerated young men? Will you stay in the slavery mind state and corrupt them more, or will you continue to be a murderer not just kill one life, but two or more lives with these detrimental thoughts? Do not buy into your own hype! This is a disaster waiting to happen! I've seen brothers go in and out of prison and they come home with these thoughts like they going to change the community.

First off, you can't change a thing until you change the condition of yourselves. Just because you have subscribed to a new way of life through religion or whatever you say has reformed you, it doesn't mean that you're cured of the same mind state that takes you in and out of prison. You are in the so-called free world where your structure will come from discipline to govern yourselves and not the daily structure you had to submit to in prison such as standing for count, eating and showering at certain times, cutting the lights out, and even being able to congregate for worship at certain times. You are not dumb just because you were incarcerated and you are not the most intelligent being just because you've been locked up for 20 to 30 years studying a religion or trade. It's easy to do right when the channels or paths to commit wrongful acts are narrow or shortened. There is nothing for you to gain by taking years out of your life being unproductive in a prison cell.

Brothers and sisters wake up and get it right! Make an affirmation today that, "I will free myself from the mental bondage and get the blessings I'm suppose to receive. You wanted to be a leader, so take this time to be a positive leader. Lead these young men and women away from the evilness they commit and submit themselves to and watch your ministry increase by overwhelming numbers. You will become one of the most prosperous reformed and rehabilitated individuals to have ever graced the prison walls. Your triumph will be your testimony. Your triumph will be your success. Your triumph will be your freedom. Your triumph will be your victory of salvation in Christ. I speak to you, because you can nurture these needy souls far better than most of us that have never seen the inside of any incarceration facility. Give yourself a chance to be free in body, mind, and spirit living beyond the walls!

Climb Out of the Pit

Psalm 40:1-3 (King James Holy Bible)

1. I waited patiently on the Lord; and he inclined unto me, and heard my cry. 2. He brought me up also out of a horrible pit, out of miry clay, and

set my feet upon a rock, and established my goings. 3. And he hath put a new song in my mouth, even praise unto our God: many shall see it, and fear, and shall trust in the LORD.

We all come by various ways to the Lord, as lumpy, unformed, beat up clay in need of the potter's hands. It is the potter that we learn, who chooses the clay he desires to work with, and transforms into a masterpiece. The clay does not choose the potter, it is the potter that looks over and places his hands on that old beat up piece of clay.

The value of one piece of clay to another is not determined by another piece of clay, but rather, it is the intrinsic value already preconceived in thought by the master potter. The master potter is Jesus, who in unison employs the Holy Spirit to send word of a change to come. The clay goes through a rigorous life of beating, pinching, poking, pulling, and sometimes even has been thrown down or slammed to the earth's most bottomed-out pit. Looking out amongst the world's congregation today, we see some pieces of clay that are crying to be lifted upon the Potter's wheel. There is a great need for believers to make affirmations and rehearse personal testimonies of once being that old broken down beat-up, lumpy, unformed, and worthless piece of clay stating, *"I've Cried My Last Cry!"*

Have you ever waited on the Lord before? You see years before my salvation, I had cried daily to the Lord. I've cried five times a day praying as a Muslim, seeking the Kingdom of Heaven on an empty promise. Having knocked and stood at a door that was locked practicing Islam, I was coming up short on Christ! The one and only mediator between man and God, known as Jehovah Jireh, now is my Lord and Savior Jesus Christ. I was crying out to the heavenly Father each time I denounced alcohol and drugs, telling God that I was a humble servant. I was crying out to the God of the Muslims, pointing out that the Christians were eating swine, drinking alcohol, committing adultery right in church, and using church as a place to trick people out of their hard earn money. My sincerity of following that way of life was tremendously set on trying to reach heaven. I thought my good works alone should have been the reward of paradise and salvation. But good works alone will not get you into the Kingdom of God! At one point in my life, I was even trying to convert my family and friends to Islam. I was seriously lost, but trying to find Jesus.

In Psalm 40 of the King James Bible, God's word reveals how David was in a horrible pit and there also appearing to be miry clay. The indication here is that not only was he found in the pit but he became sunken in the miry clay of that pit which affixed him to the bottom portion or floor of the pit. While at the bottom David is searching for a way out and inclines unto God for rescue. The plight of David's problem was found in his despair due to his sin. Not abandoning the one tool he was armed with, David trusts God and submits to offer two prayers of vindication. Knowing that his rescue is assured, David now testifies that God can be trusted.

Short of having faith, believers tend to fall short in the application of trust and prayer in the Lord Jesus Christ. We, as believers, embrace the pit as an excuse to continue to waddle in the miry clay. We seek to want people to know that we are all covered in miry clay so that they will offer sympathy for us. In all actuality, the miry clay becomes evidence of our sins. The evidence of our sins means we need cleansing. We need to be baptized in repentance however we embark upon self-betrayal and self-pity. This is where we love to cry, cry, and cry for someone to do what we can do for ourselves. God desires for us to come to Him when we are in need. God is the ladder leading out of the pit. God is the elevator and escalator that can take us from the ground floor to the top floor. All we have to due is activate that which God has already placed in us. That something is the spirit of God. The spirit of God in us is in communication with the Holy Spirit that gives us the information we need to exit the pit. Being in the pit is a temporary circumstance that receives its longevity from our unwillingness to break the chains of sins. Sin is weight. The only way to enable ourselves to climb out of the pit is to rid ourselves of the dead weight. The dead weight of sin is baggage, extra luggage, or unwanted thought processes. The Arbinger Institute (2010) defines self-betrayal in three manners: 1. An act contrary to what I feel I should do for another; 2. When I betray myself, I begin to see the world in a way that justifies my self-betrayal; and 3. When I see the world in a self-justifying way, my view of reality becomes distorted (p. 77).

When we check in at the airport to check our baggage, we are only allowed a certain number of bags that the airline will cover in the cost of our ticket. Any additional baggage or weight must be paid for prior to our bags being checked in. In other words, we cannot take flight or climb out of the pit until we have paid the cost of the heavy burdens. We cannot travel with extra baggage. Extra baggage is unpaid debt. Repentance is the payment or claim ticket for our checked in pieces of luggage. Even more important, we are only allowed limited carry-on baggage. The baggage generally consists of that which you can control in an emergency or need to maneuver upon the pilot's or flight attendant's request. Any baggage beyond this, we are made to check it in.

The word of God tells us in 1 Corinthians 10:13 of the King James Version of the Holy Bible, "No temptation has seized you except that which is common to man. And God is faithful; he will not let you be tempted beyond what you can bear. But when you are tempted, he will also provide a way out so that you can stand up under it." This tells us that God never intended for us to be in the pit. We are in the pit due to our own limitations of obedience and faith in God. The pit is merely training ground for believers to build our faith in God. The pit also challenges our intellect in the sustaining justice of God. Not only will God incline to our prayers but he has already prepared away out before we ever enter the pit. Climbing out of the pit is an act of obedience and submitting to the will of God. Our duration in the pit is a direct reflection of our untamed flesh aimlessly wondering about without spiritual guidance. We must stop screaming for help and climb out of the pit by our own confessions and obedience to the word of God.

Control the Cause of the Storm
Matthew 8:24-27 (King James Holy Bible)

24. And, behold, there arose a great tempest in the sea, insomuch that the ship was covered with the waves: but he was asleep. 25. And his disciples came to him, and awoke him, saying, Lord, save us: we perish. 26. And he saith unto them, Why are ye fearful, O ye of little faith? Then he arose, and rebuked the winds and the sea; and there was a great calm. 27. But the men marveled, saying, What manner of man is this, that even the winds and the sea obey him!

It's amazing how one dictates the environment they become part of simply because they choose to label the environment something that it's not. Most people label their environments based upon experiential events that

117

have been mislabeled by others that we become associated with through direct or indirect means. Here's where we must realize we become the cause of our own storms.

Heugens & Scherer (2010) states that in modern perspectives the organization is conceived as a tool for the efficient accomplishment of collective goals. The environment and the organization are considered to be real and separable entities that can be analyzed with the help of the sciences. The collective entities of individual dependent based elements and variables are combined in a central body or nuclei to form that which will become known as an organization.

Whenever we walk out from under the cover and concealment of protective premises and feel water making contact with our face and head, we automatically go into the rainy day mode. Those of us that have become familiar with the use of an umbrella will quickly retrieve it and any other rain gear we value as a necessity to keep us dry. We also go as far as revising our schedules because generally when it begins to rain in areas of our lives, thunder and lighting soon follows. All sorts of preconceived thoughts affect our attitudes, emotions, methods, motions, and motives. Ironically when we go back for that last piece of rain gear we happen to look out of the kitchen window and find that the sun is shining brighter than it ever has. What is happening we may stop and ask ourselves? We think back that as we opened the front door of our home, water made contact with our face and head and we turned quickly to retrieve our wet weather gear. Our attitudes, emotions, methods, motions, and motives became challenged.

Organization Theory is that branch of the social sciences that studies the design and evolution of the social structures comprising modem complex organizations, as well as the adaptation of those structures to task environments and institutional or environmental contingencies (Thompson 1967; Woodward 1965) (Heugens & Scherer, 2010). Those social sciences commend the composure of objectivity as well as satisfy the collective subjectivity of structure intended for the growth of the organization.

The aspect of a vehicle's maintenance manual is the layman methodology of the functional integration of an organization. Composed of the original parts which are identified in whole by its own entity, when injected into the makeup of the vehicle there is a functional part the item plays for the operation of the vehicle. Organization theory in comparison to a vehicle's maintenance manual allows the learner or mechanic the internal access to understand the functional parts nomenclature and specifications. Further those functional parts are and have been tested through modern, symbolic, and now are projected through sourcing of post modern perspectives to ensure the longevity of the organization or vehicle. Understanding the environment in which the organization or vehicle must operate as well as the elements and variables of society, learners, mechanics and researchers examine the dynamics of the entity for improvement. Functional integration is satisfied through all aspects of organizational theory and is therefore beneficial to the growth, productivity, and projective means of the organization.

The multiple perspectives give the learner the visual aspect of the modern makeup of predetermine rules and contracts designed to infatuate the business ethics of any given organization. Symbolic perspectives accentuate the entity of the entire organization to display the growth and ethical composition which eradicates distinct pleasures of the organizational environment from which it was created. The learner is

121

mostly influenced by postmodern perspectives as it is the summary and conducting of the previously mentioned perspectives which catapults organizations into forward mobility and success. There is the capturing of all mentally, physically, and social aspects governing change.

The typical behavior of those that have brought about their own storms has taken place. Rain does not dictate storms as fire does not dictate arson. How we assess our environments is the cause of our storms. Returning to the front door for a closer analysis of the falling water unveils that our neighbor's sprinkler system has activated and soiled our lawn. The dripping water has saturated the entrance of our dwellings. Much like the world we live in these days, we see short term with the desire for long term vision. Because of past life experiences we channel our entire thought process down one road of faith. This faith is a faith that becomes spoiled when we take on the outlook of every other person trapped in the same confines and limitations of temporary matters.

Faith is not the substance of those things controlled by the environment around the beholder. Faith is the ability to control the environment in which the beholder operates because the beholder does not focus on the storm but the one who creates the storm. Once the beholder can identify with the one that owns the storm then the beholder will understand that circumstances are always temporary. Controlling the storm has nothing to do with the change in weather or circumstances about you, it has everything to do with what you will allow yourself to become subdued by. Ships at sea that encounter storms will always fail to reach their destination when they abandon their emergency action plan and focus on the severity of the storm. People that drown do not drown because the water gets deeper, they drown because they panic after taking in small amounts of water and forget to remain calm and, and "just swim."

CHAPTER FIVE:

EVALUATE

Value Equals Vision

Proverbs 29:18 (King James Holy Bible)

18. Where there is no vision, the people perish: but he that keepeth the law, happy is he.

One of the most self-degrading links in our lives that need to be broken is the low value we see in ourselves. *The value inside of me equals the vision I pursue.* If you do not see the value in you, then don't expect anyone else to see the value in you. You will only live your life striving to achieve the biggest vision that matches the value you see in yourself. God speaks to us personally in such a way that He affirms that which we visualize from the value of the spirit of God in us. My faith confirms that God is all powerful. He will do what He says He will do. Knowing this principle and not just believing this principle, is what allows me to live out my vision. The second you intake someone else's perception of you whether it be good or bad, then you have let them place a limited value on you. Their limited value shortens your stretch to live and accomplish your vision.

Jackson (2002) reports, Western managers and HR practitioners who work with affiliates in non-Western emerging countries should particularly be aware of differences in "locus of human value (p.455)." American and other Western-based culture as it relates to human resource practices finds the importance of the bottom-line and to the shareholder value is a key issue. In wake of this view, particular challenges oppose the thought as people in their own right have developed their own value. An example of a developed culture following this perspective is Japan. Human resource practices in Japan recognize people as an integral part of their organization as well as provide a directional objective which also results in a positive effect on the organization as a whole.

Mark 12:41-44 (ESV) reads, And he sat down opposite the treasury and watched the people putting money into the offering box. Many rich people put in large sums. And a poor widow came and put in two small copper coins, which make a penny. And he called his disciples to him and said to them, "Truly, I say to you, this poor widow has put in more than all those who are contributing to the offering box. For they all contributed out of their abundance, but she out of her poverty has put in everything she had, all she had to live on."

Before you take the first step anywhere close to beginning to achieve your vision, you must ask yourself, "out of what I have, am I willing to give all that I have to achieve all that I desire?" If you only see value in the things you have at the present then you can never achieve the things you desire. The value in the things you have presently should be priceless in giving them up to receive more than the value they have sustained. Time and people will always be things you lose in the effort to accomplish your vision. People will never understand the passion you possess and you will never get back the time that you have already wasted trying to accommodate people that say they support your vision, but really don't. If you value your vision then your vision should reflect the value of you departing the worthlessness of people, thoughts, and things in your life.

The value of Jesus, the beholder of the promise of Heaven made every disciple give up their worldly lives in order to receive the Kingdom of God. They all saw a greater good, a greater value in the life of the One that could and did give us all the gift of salvation. Your vision must be attached to a greater purpose so the value of what's in you will always equal the value you seek to accomplish. How you care for people will affect your value. Also, the virtue of your life must be a fitting example of Christ, the One who loves out of the love of His Father.

There are two important values that we should keep confined in our hearts. We must exercise an *ethic of care* and an *ethic of virtue*. Velasquez (2012) defines ethic of care as one that emphasizes the value of human relationships and caring for the well-being of those who are dependent upon us (p. 76). The ethic of virtue is based on evaluations of moral character of persons or groups (Velasquez, 2012, p. 76).

We must focus on our relationships with people and not focus on our idea of the relationship. Sometimes we place our perspectives on what the relationship is or should be and never reflect upon the perspective perceived or received by the other person or persons.

Our virtues can also be misplaced as our morals sometimes conflict the present situation we face. Often times we may find value in something only as its seen through our eyes with no consideration of the other party. We become shaped by society and not the individualized care for the heart of the other person. We can even find ourselves giving the receiver our credentials for why they should accept the value of what we stated based upon our years of experience and living in something. If we are to take this perspective into life then we will always fall short in our delivery and care of people. Our virtue should include the totality of human care as per individualized assessment and not the masses. We are all shaped by our traditional ethics and morals and they sometimes come in heavy conflict with our public arenas and personal relationships.

Jesus came to lay down His life based upon the obedience to the Father. Jesus never once looked at the color, creed, gender, nationality, etc of the people. His deed was for the greater good of every man. Our identity in Jesus Christ reveals three distinctive securities which our value equals our true vision. First, Ephesians 1:6…God the Father is praised for selecting us by His mercies. Second, Ephesians 1:12…God the Son is praised for securing us by His mediation. Lastly, Ephesians 1:14 God the Holy Spirit is praised for sealing us by His ministry.

Once we connect with this value with our vision, we can begin to forward progress in accomplishing our goals. The value of our vision is increased by the determination of our heart to ascertain the desires of our spirit. Let us live with purpose and value the visionary in us all.

Present Your Best Character

2 Peter 1:5-7 (King James Holy Bible)

5. And beside this, giving all diligence, add to your faith virtue; and to virtue knowledge; 6. And to knowledge temperance; and to temperance patience; and to patience godliness; 7. And to godliness brotherly kindness; and to brotherly kindness charity.

Many have and will argue that young men grow up to be just like their fathers, even when they are known addicts, alcoholics, drunks, drug dealers, hustlers, pimps, etc. I beg to differ on the basis that it is every person's "choice" to choose the path in which they engage. Yes! I am very aware that a child born and reared in these critical situations are more likely to follow the poor leadership handed down to them by their fathers or families. At some point in life we all enter a phase of adulthood through age and not necessarily mentality, where we began to make blatant "choices." This is the time when we have to create a template for what we plan to achieve.

Set some short term goals. Short term goals are ideas that you view as obtainable in the near future. Long term goals are those ideas that you view as needing some intense ground work and knowledge to accomplish through time.

Make strong affirmations of whatever goals and oaths you choose to partake. Affirmations are statements you confirm and declare to be true and will uphold. Say what you mean, and most of all mean what you say. Be a man of your word. Your word should be bond. It's a direct reflection of your character when you break your word to another brother or sister. Don't be known as a liar, be the one everyone can count on. Don't get in over your head. Don't let your mouth project more than what you are capable of providing the means for. You will be looked at as admirable when you do this. If you bite off more than you can chew, people will look at you as not being a leader capable of completing your mission. Keep your people informed and lookout for their welfare. Make your people apart of the resolution and solution to the problem.

One character default I find in young men today is their appearance. I've been searching to find a real reason to understand who started the "pants sagging off your behind" fashion. Being a former Corrections Officer, I've always understood that style came from new inmates received in the institution that became the property of other male inmates. Yes, I did say the property of another man. Yes that's slavery but that's what you choose or chose. This new inmate is labeled a "fish". The new fish is a receiver in sex acts. The male in the relationship will even lone his fish out for sexual favors to other inmates to pay off debts owed. Every type of sexual act you can imagine performing with a female is enjoined and enjoyed by these male inmates with the new fish. Is this the character of person you are striving to achieve?

The character of a lady or woman, whichever you choose to envision, is godly. Just a few, but definitely not finite, words such as beautiful, gracefulness, loving, tenderness, virtuous, wholesome, etc come to mind when we think of what we believe are great characteristics of a good woman. I was brought up in the 70's and what I saw as respectable mothers, aunts, sisters, or women period, were those characteristics mentioned in the previous statement. Nowadays, I struggle with being upset because young ladies and ladies are the farthest thing from my expectations of a lady or true woman. I'm not afraid to say it, yes, I said my expectations. First, you must come to the understanding in me saying that, I'm speaking up for you ladies and not against you ladies.

A stroll through the mall can bring to life just where I sit with this thought. The number of young ladies timberland-out, fitted cap wearing, tattoos covering every exposed part of her body, baggy pants sagging, foul-mouth speaking, and gangsta-ed out if that's what they call it really hurts me to my heart. These are beautiful young ladies that have down played their true character to take on some misguided worldly perception. Yes, you do have the right in this worldly led time to do as you choose but why? We as men adore you. We do not wish to see your feminine character mixed with our masculine output as we are already seeing a lot of our men losing their identity or character. Maybe no one or rather the right person has told you "I love you and I do care for you!" Well yes, "I love you and I do care for you and that's what any true man would say to you with no lust to violate you.

Your character is everything! The character of a woman is priceless. The nature of a woman is priceless. Women are battling daily trying to find themselves just as well as men. I understand that the world has personified the top-ten model as a figure that you should live up to instead the righteous woman of God however that should not stop you from presenting your best character. Your character is the essence of what gives you your uniqueness. You don't need make-up, hair extensions, or fancy purses to give you value. You don't need all the falsehoods of this world to bring your value down either. You think you are leading when you really have chosen to follow the trend of people that are destroying who you really are. Sure, beautify yourself, we men love it. However, we prefer to walk hand in hand with the tenderness of God's creation that looks and sounds like who she was created to be.

2 Peter 1:5-7 is a call to believers to let their living support their faith with virtue. Believers must provide certain things to support their faith. Your identity in being born male and female is not enough. We are to live our lives with certain qualities that capture the essence of our godly characters. We must make every effort to live purposeful lives to supplement our faith with virtue. Being virtuous is not just a woman characteristic but that of a man as well. Love and patience are much desired characteristics that the world needs to uphold much more in our living with and dealing with people. There is an ever pressing need for our characters to be grounded in temperance or self-control. Temperance represents the aspect of "knowing thyself." These together empower individuals and collectively gives persons strength and endurance to run

the good race. These are also the distinguishing factors that account for fruitful human beings. It is in Jesus Christ that we should live and prosper with the Gospel.

Pray Before Time

Psalms 32:6 (King James Holy Bible)

6. For this shall every one that is godly pray unto thee in a time when thou mayest be found: surely in the floods of great waters they shall not come nigh unto him.

The most truthful of speech is the Word of God and the best guidance is the guidance of his messengers. The worst of affairs are those that are fabricated. Everything which is fabricated is an innovation. Every innovation is a going-astray, and every going-astray leads to destruction.

There is a time in life, when one must sit and think. Destruction and demoralization of society surround us. It is especially hard for those of us who, at this present moment live with hypocrisy. In these times we must remain strong. We must know that The Creator would not leave us to wait in vain. We must know that The Creator only allows us to face the difficulties of a test, and the test should bring us closer to Him. God has given our family to us as a trial, yet also as a blessing. This is why the institution of marriage is so important.

Sometimes when we face difficulties, we may feel that the mercy and love of God has left us. In these thoughts we are wrong. God only wishes to purify us through trials and tribulations. Through these tests, God willing, we become stronger in faith. We become closer to God. Every believer will continuously be tested. With every difficulty comes a time of ease.

We must continue to seek guidance, love and mercy from The Creator only. There is no other that can guide us and keep us safe from the evils created by our own hands. We must keep our dreams of freedom alive. We must not give up hope that one day we will be blessed with a peaceful life.

We must not be afraid to lose our temporal lives to obtain eternal freedom. In these times of trials and tribulations, God has provided for us families. Either they can help us to become closer to The Creator or they can take us away. If they attempt to take us away from God, then we should take action. We should not let anyone, not even family destroy the most important relationship that we have. Our relationship with The Creator is most valuable.

There is a choice to be made by all, to worship

God or worship our desires. Prayer, peace and worldly mischief cannot co-exist. We were all born with a common purpose of serving and we should only worship The Creator. By knowing our purpose in life, we are better prepared. We know why we are here, and we know why we exist. With a clear perception of where we are, we have a better understanding of life, and despair is erased from the mind. Life has new meaning and we thank The Creator for every breath we take, and for each and every opportunity we have to worship and serve him. Amen.

Visualize the Victory

I John 5:4 (King James Holy Bible)

4. For whatsoever is born of God overcometh the world: and this is the victory that overcometh the world, even our faith.

Leaders visualize the victory beyond the battle. Most teams enter their seasons dreaming of making it to the big dance. Everyone dreams of making it to the championship. Each season comes and goes and winners are crowned for the title. How do you suppose the losers feel? How do you suppose the winners prepared themselves? The even more important question one might ask is, "Did they really prepare to win the title or did they prepare to get to play for the title?"

This level of thinking is what separates leaders from wanna-be leaders? The practice courts, fields, halls,

144

and etc. are filled with exclamations of excitement, hopes, and promises to work hard to get to the big show. Visions of hysterical fans and stadiums, filled with entertainment and music, awaiting the singing of the various National Anthems, are the visual aspects of the celebrated claim to fame. Society teaches us that practice makes perfect. When in reality, routine practices sharpen your game play. There is no such perfect practice and there is no such perfect game. The more proficient you are in practice and games, the better your chances are for wining any given game. The effort that is put into practices should spill over into game play.

If you are only practicing and playing to get to the championship, then what will you do when you get to the championship? It is apparent that you have reached your goal. Just ask the members of the Buffalo Bills and the Denver Broncos, who both went to Superbowls four times without victories. What do you believe was their shortcomings? One could argue that penalties and poor play execution were the causes, but I stand on the fact that they didn't plan at the beginning of the season to win the Superbowls. One year after another, they ran the race to get back to the Superbowl to prove to themselves they were winners, but the win was not visualized. Did they not think about the numerous games they played trampling teams as they drove through the schedule defeating team after team? Something had to happen different! Someone had to take charge and become a leader that visualized the victory before the battle.

Denver Broncos were now about to embark on the concept of visualizing the victory before the battle. Having played in six Superbowls, their first being in 1978, with a loss to the Dallas Cowboys 27-10, the Broncos would see the big dance five more times. In

1997, the emerging leader came in the form of Terrell Davis, Denver's running back and Superbowl MVP, who led Denver to a 31-24 victory over the Green Bay Packers. In 1998, the emerging leader, who played in five of Denver's Superbowls and crowned MVP was John Elway, Denver's quarterback. The Broncos were able to take home back to back titles with a victory over the Atlanta Falcons 34-19. This was subsequently the same year John Elway retired.

You have to have seen both of these players in action through the years they won their Superbowl MVP awards. Each player made it his personal vendetta and spread the wealth among their team to visualize Superbowl wins. Getting to the Superbowl was no more than just another game to the four time losers of Superbowls. Something had to be done different. If you want something different, then you have to do something different. The results of the

Superbowl victories came when the MVP players figuratively speaking, put their team on their back and led them to a victory. Sure it was a team effort, but the victory was visualized first through a leader and then mirrored upon the team. When you want something better, you have to do something better. When you play for a greater cause, then you play with a greater effect.

Visualizing the victory beyond the battle ensures that you and your team are focused on all that is required to secure success. No one can conceivably conquer when they have not perceived the victory. A challenger faces a champion with doubt in their minds. The champion needs only to show up and make a strong appearance. The challenger must first visualize the win in order to conquer all doubts of his or her quest to conquer the giant. A well organized platoon of 50 men can easily defeat an unorganized group of 100 men.

Carelessly unorganized individuals move forward in battle, while skilled warriors plan counter-attacks.

This question was once proposed to me. If a king had a kingdom full of all his worldly riches and it came under attack, with me being the king's chief warrior, and I had to engage in battle against one group of enemies, which would I engage in battle with? One force would be led by a sheep with herds of lions and the other would be led by a lion with herds of sheep. Which would I engage as to posing the worst threat? I ask you to answer the question. I chose to engage the lion who led the herds of sheep. Now let me explain my answer, because the person who asked me the question couldn't believe I answered it correctly.

Visualize a sheep leading herds of lions. There is most definitely a significant flaw in that. If you have a sheep leading herds of lions, then what does that say about the lions? Don't be fooled by thinking because

149

the sheep is weaker, he must have some good leadership skills. Lions will never follow sheep unless to eat him. A lion leading a herd of sheep displays a strong leader and one that has instilled strength in his flock or herds. Truly the lion leading the sheep would be my choice of engagement. They pose the greatest danger to the king's kingdom.

If you had to entrust a wolf or a fox, which would you trust? I would trust the wolf, because there would be no doubt in my mind that he would be out to get me. The fox, on the other hand, would be clever and conniving, insisting he is my friend. He would genuinely win the trust of many, while secretly planning to eat you at his first chance. You wouldn't let the wolf get close enough to even smell you.

Visualizing the victory beyond the battle will ultimately ensure that you examine all possibilities that are detrimental to your existence. Leaders will walk, while followers rush in unknowingly falling to unknown danger. The Bible tells us that the steps of a righteous man are ordered by God. We do not go before God and nor do we make decisions without God's consulting through prayer. God has authored this life mysteriously beyond the capabilities of our deepest thoughts. The battles for which we concern ourselves are but particles of milestones crumbled under God's hand. The Creator of all is the master consultant for any strategic matter that could be fathomed. We don't dance with the devil, however we do waltz to the melody of God's Word.

CHAPTER SIX:

DEVELOP

Develop the Will to Do

Philippians 2:12-13 (King James Holy Bible)

12. Wherefore, my beloved, as ye have always obeyed, not as in my presence only, but now much more in my absence, work out your own salvation with fear and trembling. 13. For it is God which worketh in you both to will and to do of his good pleasure.

Spiritual leaders often times witness the lack of congregational obedience in their absences. However in Paul's absence, this was not the conduct of the Philippians for the most part. Scripture encourages us to keep on working diligently in the absence of our spiritual leaders towards the goal of our desired results. Divine sovereignty and human freedom is a blessing in the cooperation of those to work in spite of. We work out of freedom and responsibility.

So many of us boys and men lack the will to do, but run with the desire to want. We lack the will to do and therefore our inner ambitions are scarred by the very lackluster performances we display.

Let's examine this nature. As we live day in and day out, we began to develop a worldly spirit of wanting the most materialistic desires of our hearts. For young boys, they may desire the new X-Box, PSP, Nintendo, PlayStation, NBA or NFL jerseys and/or sneakers, while the men may desire the newest Mercedes Benz, BMW, Michael Kors or Invicta watches, tallest rims for their vehicles, etc., all out of the wanting spirit. Now ask yourselves how many of you have actually put a plan in effect that will allow you to achieve these things.

For young boys, there are many chores that you can turn into entrepreneurial tools. Before you can turn these chores into entrepreneurial tools, you must first have the initiative and motivation to act responsible. Initiative is defined as ability to act on your own: the ability to act and make decisions without the help or advice of other people; introductory step: the first step in a process that, once taken, determines subsequent events; plan: a plan or strategy designed to deal with a particular problem. Motivation is defined as internal and external factors that stimulate desire and energy in people to be continually interested in and committed to a job, role, or subject, and to exert. Motivation is also defined as to give reason, incentive, enthusiasm, or interest that causes a specific action or certain behavior.

Chores such as cutting grass, delivering newspapers, cutting hedges, washing widows, raking yards, and washing cars are entrepreneurial tools that will afford you the resources of revenue to acquire those desired materialistic things. Young boys you cannot live this life thinking that someone will be giving you the desires of your heart if you lie on your backsides and do nothing. Nothing makes a mother or father prouder than knowing that their young boys have taken the initiative to take out the trash and cut grass, without having to be told to do so. The first step in becoming a leader is acting upon the characteristics and actions of a positive and effective role model, displaying leadership traits. Don't run from leadership that urges you to have some "get up and go" about yourself. There were many times in my life as a young man where I had to assist my cousins in their chores at the call of my uncle. I thought that was overboard, but my uncle was teaching me to be a man in these instances. I couldn't see it at that time because I felt like that was their home and responsibility and my chores were complete. My uncle wasn't free from mistakes, but rest assured that didn't stop him from being a father to many young men in our neighborhood. He taught me how to step in and be a man helping others, especially in the instances where women lacked fathers to teach their boys to be men.

Men, we know we have tremendous desires of the heart that are often triggered by what we see on television, what we see our neighbors acquire, or just wanting something so we can say we were the first to get it. Have we really put a needs plan in effect? Assess your needs and wants by developing a list separating the two categories. More often times in men that are not business men, we tend to see outrageous output focused on wants or desires. The needs category is usually significantly smaller than the wants category. Some of us really think we are leaders and find out through self-examination tests that we are mostly followers. I remember being employed as a Deputy Sheriff some years ago. I went out and purchased a motorcycle because it was something that I had desired for quite a while. Yes it was an extreme desire, because financially it was a bad move, but I maintained my desire. Not until I had an accident did the other deputies realize that I had a motorcycle. The funny thing about it was that, after I went out and replaced my motorcycle with a new one, it was then the trend started. It was even at that point that most of the deputies had already possessed Four Wheel ATVs. It was even suggested that I should get a four wheeler. I felt like that was going backwards from a motorcycle to an ATV, but I must admit that I did entertain the thought, by actually checking into buying an ATV. That was a very short lived thought, because I couldn't afford to buy it straight out and I had too much responsibility to get one financed for another payment. All on the efforts of getting a motorcycle, one deputy borrowed money to buy a motorcycle that he ended up not liking too much, once he rode with the ones of us that rode sports bikes or "crotch-rockets". As time

158

went on, the deputies began fishing a lot. This led from one deputy having a boat and then others going out doing whatever they could to get a boat. As even more time went on, I left the Sheriff Department and pickup trucks became a fad. Now all the deputies began to buy pickup trucks. Now, understand that some of them had some really nice looking trucks, and I'm not putting them down, but I knew how much deputies made in the small county where I worked and it was ridiculously not affordable. They were able to acquire them by whatever means so I'm not knocking them. However, was this leadership or the attitude of a follower? This was definitely the attitude of a follower. A real leader would have been more in tuned to family financial matters, as nearly all of us were married with children. Some of us even developed selfish attitudes as we went out and bought everything we wanted and the family was put on hold for their wants. If you can relate to this type of behavior, then sad enough to say, you are a follower.

A man assesses his family's needs and then takes care of himself. Let's back up for a second, of course he ensures he has been taken care of mentally and physically, but he then is responsible for the care and protection of his family. All his family needs and even desires are taken in consideration prior to fulfilling any of his materialistic wants. A real man feels great about caring, protecting, and providing for his family, even though, he hasn't rewarded himself. We have to develop "the will to do," so that we will enable the boys that we are responsible for leading, will pass on these very much needed acts of leadership. If you want to cripple a nation, all you have to do is cripple the man and watch the nation crumble.

The man seems to run with a spirit for wanting to be recognized by acts that catapult him into a world of appraisal and honor. This can be seen as our braggadocios ego. If men are the leaders of a nation, then why is it that our focus is on all that matters the least? We tend to focus on women with big butts, beautiful smiles, and a well endowed chest. We don't focus on family and children. Is it that we are scared of responsibility and/or we feel that this life is merely just a time for alcohol and partying? I can tell you my brothers, you will never lose women chasing the leadership of being an entrepreneur, but you will always lose positions of leadership and money chasing women. Let's be about our business and mold more responsible leaders that will run with the will to do, and leave alone the desires and wants that will affect our growth of leadership.

Delete Your "Plan B"?

Psalms 31:24 (King James Holy Bible)

24. Be of good courage, and he shall strengthen your heart, all ye that hope in the Lord.

Why do you need a "B" Plan when you say you are planning to be successful? I can't remember one time in my life when my mother has ever encouraged me to have a "B" Plan. I do remember my mother telling me lots of times, to pray and give it my all. I do not know where this thought even manifested itself. When I hear this statement, I immediately think that the person saying this is merely side tracked by having their thoughts spread out over two or more plans. So then I would have to ask them if they are really focusing on their goal.

Many years ago, I remember watching a television interview featuring Denzel Washington. In the interview, Denzel Washington was asked how his illustrious career started. I hung on every word that Denzel stated, being that I saw him as a man who had climbed to the top of the success ladder through hard work and dedication to his craft and goals. The one thing that stood out more than anything in the interview was when the interviewer asked him, what was his Plan "B" if being an actor failed? You should have seen Denzel's face! He looked puzzled, but with a serious facial expression. He then replied, I didn't have a Plan "B"! He further stated that it was his belief that if he had been planning a Plan "B", then he wasn't planning to be successful. I immediately thought to myself, that's like the realest thing I've ever heard any actor or successful person say. Now, I don't have to tell you how successful Denzel Washington has been on the screen and in his family life. I just know as well as you do that the number of leading roles he has played through the years have been in movies that movie goers

stand in line for at the Box Office. Whenever a movie

is advertising and you see Denzel's face on the scene,

you immediately say, "Oh, I have to go see that!"

God has an impeccable credibility that we all should

stand in line for. With God you don't need a Plan B.

God should be our primary plan of living. If we all

press towards the mark of the higher calling there is no

Plan B to achieve. We cannot drive full speed ahead if

we never take the vehicle out of reverse. We have to

stop spinning wheels in doubt of ourselves claiming

that we are trusting God. You cannot pacify your true

desires with Plan B materialism. Your true desires can

and will only be fulfilled with the unmatched Hand of

God.

Let's examine the Plan "B"! Plan "B" is developed

immediately after you state what your goal is. You

really can't say that you've made an affirmation

towards your goal, because in stating your goal, you say, but my Plan "B" is going to be this or that. Now how much effort and energy have you put into your Plan "A"?

If an architectural designer is setting out to construct the most elegant home known to man, he must first conceptualize the idea of the elegant home. He must then gather his research and resources to construct such a home. Do you think that in the middle of him striving to build this one of a kind masterpiece, that he lifts his pencil to start work on the blueprint for building an outside barn? That's right, I said an outside barn! If it sounds ridiculous, then it should. The same distraction it took from the masterpiece is the same distraction you face when striving to accomplish your goals and right in the middle of your hard work and dedication, you take time out to go build a barn. Now ask yourself, have you really planned to succeed?

Dr. Daniel Hale Williams was the first African American, who performed the first successful open heart surgery. Think to yourself and see if you can fathom the thought of him being so focused on performing this miracle known to man, and right at the height of the surgery, he looks to his assistants and starts expressing his desire to build a race car and race in the Indianapolis 500, if the open-heart surgery fails. Where is his focus? You can clearly see that a Plan "B" will not work when working diligently on your goal.

This is like striving to do right, but planning to do wrong in the same instance. It can't be done. You will have to give focus to one or the other. If your goal is to do right, then you have to develop the mindset and research other ways to keep you moving towards accomplishing your goal. You will not have time to worry about failing.

Plan "B" planners must know that the "B" signifies "Bombing Out"! This is disastrous. I'm not saying that you don't take precautions, but I am saying that you don't have time as a leader to plan to fail. You are depending on yourself and Plan "B" relays the message of doubt. For a person with belief, this is acting on faith and moving forward knowing that you have done and are doing everything you can possibly do to succeed. This means that you are asserting and exerting every ounce of energy you can into your goal. A determined leader is one that plans for success and achieves success. If you factor in a Plan "B", then you will achieve a Plan "B". Goals should never be set to fail. These should be strong affirmations of a confident leader.

Eggs in One Basket

Isaiah 10:14 (King James Holy Bible)

14. And my hand hath found as a nest the riches of the people: and as one gathered eggs that are left, have I gathered all the earth; and there was none that moved the wing, or opened the mouth, or peeped.

The very first thing I wish for you to get in your mind is this simple affirmation. Say this and say it out loud at the top of your voice… "I'm not saving anymore eggs! I'm putting them all in the basket!" That's it you are now ready. Your next move is a calculation of breaking through the suppressed desires. You hold the key to your next promotion but you keep holding back. You hold the key to enjoying the limitless joy you want in your marriage. You hold the keys to that unconditional love for your family members. You hold the key to that new house, that new car, that new job, that new life, but you just will not put all your eggs in the basket.

Who have you allowed to tell you not to give your all? Better yet, why have you allowed them to limit your potential? Why are you so comfortable with complaining about not getting what you deserve but you keep holding back from depositing every little bit of resources that you have. You're not hungry enough to want the next level. You're not invested enough in your marriage because "momma-and-them" have told you to not trust and not give it all to your marriage because they failed miserably from being instructed the correct way.

Hello Mr. or Mrs. Could-have-been the CEO but I didn't put that one small job detail on my resume because "THEY" told me it wasn't important. What will it take for you to break these yokes? What will it take for you to break out of these chains that you invite to enslave you? Why are you holding on to eggs that will tip the basket into your favor?

You have left one or two eggs in your nest and cannot benefit from them because you are more focused on storing up riches instead of putting all your resources into being the success you wish to be. You cannot trust God and pray if you don't make it at the same time. Either you must trust God that regardless the outcome you'll still be blessed or you will not trust Him at all. Your faith has to be increased, your physical has to be decreased, and God has to increase.

Holding onto eggs places you in the same position as the man that buried his talent because he only had one and the others had two and five. What you do with your talents (eggs) will be the life or death of you. God is waiting to see if you're going to keep hiding your eggs or sew your eggs. Are you looking for fruit or unfertile land? Eggs are just eggs until they are nurtured and protected. Once they have been properly cared for they will bring forth a product. Yes the product is hatched and in return produces more eggs that give birth to more product.

You have to sew all your seeds in order to reap the fruit. We never know which seed is the seed that will bring forth fruit but one thing we do know is if we don't plant them all we stand the chance of holding onto the one that may have given us life. Countless people have latched onto this concept of not putting all their eggs in one basket and no one can really tell them that it produced a greater result. They can only tell you that they failed because they held on to a few eggs and used those for their "Plan B." No! Their "Plan B" was actually eggs out of their "Plan A" but they don't realize it because they were more focused on doubt and not succeeding the first time around. Honestly their minds were more set for failure than wired for success.

Not putting your eggs in one basket is much like creating a "Plan B". This is another one of those sayings that I'm not sure where the origin began. I tend to think of the supposed Easter Bunny when it comes to putting your eggs in one basket. Now, I think it's important to know that a bunny or a rabbit is a warm blooded mammal, which does not give birth through the process of laying eggs. Chickens lay eggs. Cats and dogs have babies much like mammals known as humans. So the entire thought of rabbits laying eggs is "out-the-window."

We're back to the thought of giving your all, to be what it is you choose to be. Most of us have probably heard another statement about not spreading yourself too thin. Let's think about a rubber band? A rubber band in its composure is a strong material. When stretched to its end, the rubber band becomes compromised and very much in danger of breaking.

When the bands or belts in your transmission become overly stretched or worn, your transmission starts to slip. This means that no matter how much acceleration you give the vehicle, it still remains in the same position.

You, being that transmission, will work for the purpose of moving yourself towards accomplishing a goal or goals set but you will remain in the same position. Now, using the eggs, which we will call your resources, you must use every vital part it takes to secure a perfectly working transmission to get you moving towards your goals. If you have the resources to properly secure a practically brand new or remanufactured transmission, why would you hold back on using every resource or material you have to fix your transmission? If you are really expecting the transmission to properly work, then you must use every resource that you have to ensure that you are successful in purchasing or rebuilding the transmission. Were you planning to fix the transmission, while at the same time hoping it didn't work? I do not believe that would have been your thought.

Real leaders cannot afford not to give their all nor use every resource they have to accomplish a mission. A real leader would equip his people and himself with the resources to meet those unexpected situations which usually occur. Preparing for the worst is a great practice in leadership. No matter what you plan to do in this life, you have to put your eggs in one basket. If you choose to hold back on putting all your eggs in one basket, then you are setting out to fail, just like creating a "Plan B". It's real hard to believe that a person would genuinely go on a hike through a desert, which requires three water-filled canteens, with no stops for water, and leave two of his water-filled canteens behind, in case he's thirsty when he returns. I don't know about you, but from my military experiences and field training, all three canteens (eggs) are going with me, when I travel across that desert. What good would the two canteens be to you, which you left behind, if you're not going to make it back?

Simply stated, it would behoove you to put all your eggs into one basket, knowing that you are giving your all and exhausting every means of resource afforded to you. A farmer cannot truthfully say that he is sure that his crops are beyond growing on land that he refuses to cultivate and use his new John Deere tractor. If his old tractor is not dispensing seeds in the proper manner needed to place the seeds in the soil, and he refuses to use his new tractor until his old tractor completely breaks down, then he has chosen not to put all his eggs into one basket. Yes, he has chosen not to plant products to grow to fruitful produce. He is spreading his eggs thin awaiting his old tractor to breakdown, when in all actuality, he over looked the fact that

regardless of the tractor not being completely broken,

he had the necessary tools to plant a fruitful field but

chose not to exert or exhaust all his resources (eggs).

Do not plan to fail, by failing to plan! Use your eggs

wisely and benefit from using your entire stock.

Reserved energy needed is wasted energy, if not used

when needed!

"No intimate relationships should begin until you sacrifice yourself for greater expectations of your personal goals. Plan your future based upon your level of commitment to obtain your goals and not fantasizing the status of someone else."

~Dr. Aqeel Taahir Ash-Shakoor, CDKA~

CHAPTER SEVEN:

MATURE

Grow Amongst the Weeds

Matthew 13:29-30 (King James Holy Bible)

29. But he said, Nay; lest while ye gather up the
tares, ye root up also the wheat with them. 30. Let both
grow together until the harvest: and in the time of
harvest I will say to the reapers, Gather ye together first
the tares, and bind them in bundles to burn them: but
gather the wheat into my barn.

A seed is that part of the plant which is produced by
means of sexual reproduction bearing an embryo and
produces new life. The problem with most of us is that
we know that we are seeds but we fail to understand
that we have the ability to grow amongst weeds. We
have latched on and become attached to older seeds that
failed to receive the nurturing from the air, sun, and
water that God has provided. As seeds, we were thrown
into a hole preparing us to sprout. As I tackle this from

the start, I will not waste time telling you that the one

that placed you in the pit did not place you there

expecting you to grow. The trial of the pit was a place

where you were to establish your identity and grow to

your purpose.

An organism is defined as a form of life composed of

mutually interdependent parts that maintain various

vital processes. Morgan (2006, p. 33) states we think of

organizations as living systems existing in a wider

environment on which they depend for the satisfaction

of various needs.

"In the process, organization theory has become a

kind of biology in which the distinctions and relations

among *molecules, cells, complex organisms, species,*

and *ecology* are paralleled in those between *individuals,*

groups, organizations, populations (species), of

organizations, and their *social ecology* (Morgan, 2006,

p. 34)." Jobs and interpersonal relations are comparable

to organisms and their environments in so much that the environment is crucial to an organism's growth.

As we are forming in our embryonic stage, the interval of time from fertilization, you must know who you are before you sprout to where the world may identify you. As we reach maturity and peak through the soil of the world, life as we come to know it begins. What is not so apparent is that during the time we were out of the spotlight or in the earth, weeds were entangling themselves to our roots. These were the doubters, the hypocrites, the naysayers, and an entire dimension of entities attacking you at conception plotting your destiny to be what they were too scared to grow to.

The needs of individuals, groups, and organizations must all be satisfied. Morgan (2006, p. 38) implies, it is this kind of thinking that now underpins the "open systems approach" to organization, which takes its main inspiration from the work of Ludwig von Bertalanffy, a theoretical biologist. Developed simultaneously on both sides of the Atlantic in the 1950s and 1960s, the systems approach builds on the principle that organizations, like organisms, are "open" to their environment and must achieve an appropriate relation with that environment if they are to survive.

This theory holds true as we look at the living organisms known as plants. In order for a plant to grow and flourish, we must first ensure that the plant is grown in the right area for healthy nurturing. We must have the plant rooted in the proper soil, spacing for growth, alignment to receive water, and proper placement to receive light or a source of heat. Without the availability of these variables, the plant will surely die. Organizations viewed as organisms are much alike. Organizations are properly constructed with variables such as designs of the business/buildings, location, population of the environment, accessibility, compatibility of services needed, etc. all taken in account for the organization's existence and longevity.

We could take the approach as the unskilled gardener and pluck all the weeds but just as the biblical context warns us about tares, we learn a more valuable lesson of maturity. We don't have to pull up or destroy the weeds in order for us to grow to our potential. What we must learn to do is not focus on the weeds and focus on what feeds us and gives us nourishment. Roadblocks are designed to keep you from going down paths where bridges are out or roads are under construction. Those of us focusing on the bridge being out will become sidetracked and stuck in traffic instead of taking the detour road that provides safety towards your intended direction.

Once we focus on our mission, then we know that there are more avenues of approach than those that are closed down where weeds have grown through the pavement. When your foundation is solid not even weeds can interrupt your composition. In fact, the more you grow the better you will look with weeds wrapped around your trunk. Your value will be intrinsic and proving not to querulous behavior. Seeds with purpose in their lives do not affix themselves to excuses why they can't grow in certain circumstances. Just remember that as seeds grow, they do not stay seeds, they become beautiful plants that need repotting because they have outgrown their environment. Is God repotting you now or have you chosen to become a weed and hinder the growth of others that have chosen to soar? Your capability to grow does not rest in the ability of the weeds to strangle you. CPR or Cardio Pulmonary Respiration is performed when something

184

has given up or died and needs restoring. Fertile seeds do not need CPR; they need CRP…Constant Reminding of Purpose!

Grow Beyond Your Traditions
Matthew 15: 1-6 (King James Holy Bible)

Then came to Jesus scribes and Pharisees, which were of Jerusalem, saying, 2.Why do thy disciples transgress the tradition of the elders? for they wash not their hands when they eat bread. 3. But he answered and said unto them, Why do ye also transgress the commandment of God by your tradition? 4. For God commanded, saying, Honour thy father and mother: and, He that curseth father or mother, let him die the death. 5. But ye say, Whosoever shall say to his father or his mother, It is a gift, by whatsoever thou mightest be profited by me; 6. And honour not his father or his mother, he shall be free. Thus have ye made the commandment of God of none effect by your tradition.

We are creatures of habit! We are molded by our broken perspectives of repetitive actions that duplicate the original action. Each time we duplicate that which has already been duplicated, we lose those small tenets of quality although it appears just as sharp as the original. As long as we duplicate then we can never generate new life or opportunity.

Morgan (2006) quotes Marshall McLuhan, noting that "the last thing a fish is likely to discover is the water it is swimming in" (p. 209). Water is so central to the fish and its way of life that the water goes unseen and taken for granted. Our personal perspectives of life are very similar in this regard. In analyzing the fish metaphor, the notion is that we neglect spiritual freedom and embrace the natural submitting to psychic prisons.

One of the great things I love doing is listening to great preachers who drive a sermon like a safari vehicle. From the very moment they pull up and you board the vehicle it becomes an adventure. You get the full experience. However if I, as a preacher, would duplicate the same sermon without giving experiences in my own tongue the intrinsic value will be loss over time. There would be a lack of response yielding motivation to change. This happens to us all that choose not to push the envelope to break traditions. Traditions are called traditions because we directly and indirectly have made ourselves comfortable with the first feeling that overwhelmed us and was produced from some event. Life does not bring about change, people bring about change.

Morgan (2006) suggests in times of change it is possible to look at almost any industry and find once successful firms struggling to survive. In 1982, Tom

Peters and Robert Waterman wrote about excellent companies such as IBM. By the 1990s, many were struggling. Their particular style of excellence had become a trap that prevented them from thinking in new ways and from transforming themselves to meet new challenges (p. 209).

The purity of organizations is not necessarily lost in the beginning stages but more so in the later stages of expected growth period. The purity of existence heralded by organizations is patterned after the facet of fighting for survival indirectly by not focusing on growing but the need of the partakers. Essentially the organizations are created as a "meet-the-needs" of the people contributor but lose their identity and purpose through the success of the organization's performing growth. Strengths and limitations of these organizations are simultaneously produced in the same atmosphere however one not nurtured properly can be the stagnation of the other. The goal must not be abandoned in order for the strength of the organization to remain pure. Limitations are comfort zones of expected growth or operation.

Given any group of people from different ages, demographics, nationalities, race, etc. gathered in a conversation of what the proper upbringing for a child should be, we would hear all sorts of methodologies. Without giving ear to new and better methods of raising children, we would automatically retreat to our traditions and drive the point home that we have the best solution. Miraculously, the conversation would not be about improvement; it would become more about the desire to remain the same. Tradition cripples all entities. Once we become comfortable with our environment and the way we receive satisfaction, we only work towards and to the limitations of stagnation. Over time we begin to believe that we are growing or maintaining the original quality of that which was produced by those means that were available to us at that time.

Since its establishment the church has taken on many forms of purpose. The word "church" is used in modern English in reference to local congregations or assemblies and buildings and denominations. Not venturing towards the mark of "assembly" or "congregation" has misplaced the value and false teaching in the universal or invisible church. The reckless venture has negated the modern day existence of the church. Once used as a meeting place for law bearers, the church as we know it today has been falling in its true worth influenced by the precepts of a fish in water. Morgan (2006) quotes Marshall McLuhan, noting that "the last thing a fish is likely to discover is the water it is swimming in" (p. 209).

Tradition has foiled the truthfulness of the church and remanufactured its purpose with remnants of both the political and spiritual world. More so in today's time church is the organization which is aligned to provide for the spiritual needs of the people however the political tenets seem to overshadow the number one goal of the organization, "saving souls." As this overlooked water surrounding the fish continues to flow, we will find the fish belly up in the very water that it lives and swims. What was once known as a place of refuge from the evils of the world has now engulfed itself in a favorable business operation leaving all to find that the true church is not actually a building but a place within the hearts of the people. Tradition within the sacred institutions stagnate the growth because of the lack of attention given to the individual soul nurturing in lieu of generating operational funding. The very employee or patriot of the organization sees their worth or room for self-improvement more farfetched than a reality. Church is now viewed as just a regular meeting place of those with a common interest for at least a day of service. We are the proverbial fish swimming in the water not realizing the importance or intrinsic value of the church. The investment of self-worth of the people is that which grows the church and functions profitable variables of love, joy, and peace. Also, we discover that the fish is just as essential to the water as the water is to the fish.

Breaking tradition is having faith that sustains you to welcome the opportunity for growth without feeling your existence is threatened by the knowledge, wisdom, and understanding of new ideas. Principles become principles once a collective group comes together to set like ideas as the method in which they will operate. What if there was only one principle made for everyone. What if that one principle generated a commonality between all people, places, and things and followed the concept that they would all be built upon the idea that at anytime they would commit to change. Now the worst of traditional thinkers would give this reply to the previous statement…"change doesn't always mean better." Well to even have to address that means that they are traditionally looking for an excuse to remain in the same attitude and mindset of opposing the possibility of growth. Here's the thought! If you don't grow or break tradition you will die within that same condition. You can only do one thing the same way for so long before it becomes redundant and produces lackluster performance. I love the fact that the Holy Bible bears the words, "study to show thyself approved" and not read to show thyself approved.

Reading becomes redundant and generates nostalgia. That same nostalgia affects growth. Studying brings about traditional change which promotes energy or life. So when we think back to those preachers I spoke of earlier, we see that having studied their material they are able to exegesis the scriptures in such a way that they present them to you in the format of a movie. You get the full visual aspect of the scripture instead of just a well read word. Our lives are not traditionally fashioned. Each person has a special gift and or purpose designed just within them as a fingerprint that only the owner can bear. The fruits of those that grow outside the confines of the bordered garden reach their real potential on fertile land because they grow beyond their traditional potting.

Wait on Your Season

Psalms 1:1-3 (King James Holy Bible)

1. BLESSED IS the man that walketh not in the counsel of the ungodly, not standeth in the way of sinners, nor sitteth in the seat of the scornful. 2. But his delight is in the law of the Lord; and in his law doth he meditate day and night. 3. And he shall be like a tree

planted by the rivers of water, that bringeth forth his fruit in his season; his leaf also shall not wither; and whatsoever he doeth shall prosper.

I start by saying, *"God wants you to start, while the devil wants you to ride the bench!"* Wait on your season! Too many times we get caught up analyzing other's situations. Why aren't things happening for you when your friends are seemingly prospering? Why is it that you are the one conducting yourself in the most appropriate manner and making God the forefront of your life, but your friends are doing X, Y, Z and living in the lap of luxury?

I will tell you why! It is simply not your season. You see, you must first understand that your season is coming in due time. It does not come when everyone else's season is in. Do you want to reap the hell storm they had to fight in order to enjoy the pleasures they posses now? Do you think happiness comes without a price? Have you even thought that God will answer your prayers if you just continue to exercise patience, prayer, and faith? Leaders are not whiners! Leaders are not impatient beings! Leaders know that their worth is very near. Leaders further recognize that the value of what they do is not a monetary rewarding, but that of a much greater power and authority.

Understand that the authority and power from which you will be rewarded is far greater than your neighbors, because it's meant entirely for you. Had you received your neighbors reward, you wouldn't have received it well or in good spirit. The reward was not the reward of your investment. It was simply not the tenet of your labor or means.

When your season comes, you will know that it is about you in many ways. You will recognize the illumination of the authority and power that has blessed you with the coming of your season. It will be fruitful and more abundant than you could have ever imagined. You will be stunned by the capacity of joy that overwhelms your inner spirit. Your flesh will tingle with an unknowing twinge as you've never felt before. Your light will shine as the Lord has commanded you to let illuminate, so that the world will recognize the blessed ones. Your concentration will not be on the season itself, but more so the fruit it bears.

When all is seemingly at its end, reach down, dig in deep, and drive like you've never driven before. The works of your hands will match the works of your heart. The heart of gold is worthy of the most precious sentiments of the heavenly gifts. You will never fail giving your all, but you will fail not giving your all.

Your season is more than just a time in life. Your season is confirmation of a promise bestowed upon the speaking or profession of your tongue, when you just simply say, "Lord have mercy upon me!" As you continue to march on in the rainiest of rainy days," you are displaying a show of good faith and great perseverance in your troubled times. Once you condition your mind to understand that waiting on your season is much better than trying to soak up someone else's sunshine, you will then be rewarded with a season of righteously earned multitudes of favor. You are highly favored, so there is no reason not to await your season.

If we are too aggressive in demanding what we were commanded to wait on, the prosperity of that to come, will be lessened due to our impatience, hastiness, and overbearing spirits. If you were shown your blessings beforehand, how hard would you really work? It would be like being on your job and receiving a full months pay before you ever go to work. What would you do on those cold, foggy, rainy mornings of a workday? How would you feel? Would you contemplate calling out for

the day or would you treat it like you hadn't been paid?

Most people would consider calling out, because the

bed feels so good on those mornings. Now understand

that having to work for a blessing is much better. When

you receive the blessing which is your paycheck, you

are more than just happy, you are fulfilled in knowing

that you earned it.

Waiting on your season is the coming of maturity.

Maturity begins with an understanding of self. Once

you understand self, you can rationalize that nature is

the nucleus of all. Once your rationale reveals nature as

the nucleus, then you can further conceptualize the

essence of that which created all. God will not let a

good leader go unrewarded. His works always remain

fruitful. Good leaders don't have to stand around

antagonizing God with statements like, "God you said

you was going to bless if I did this and that!" Good

leaders continue performing good works and before they know it, they have more blessings than they could even use at the time, so they share their blessings with those less fortunate. This is not to be confused with thinking you can do good works to earn God's favor. The question then becomes, are you a good leader? Are you awaiting your season? Are you demanding when your season should be? When you have zeal upon you, you're not cognizant of the amount of good works you've conducted looking to receive certain blessings. Your work is habitual. Your blessings are plentiful. Your worth is priceless. Your gratitude is abundant. Your temper is calm. Your pleasure is trusting. And, your presence is forever commanded upon the flock of the Greatest Shepherd.

When trouble stirs and the light of your happiness is faced with dark clouds, energize your faith and shine even brighter. Darkness of evil will try to steal your season's fruit, but it can only be accomplished if you choose to dim your light. The source of your light is far more superior over the darkest evil that lurks to destroy your peace. Your season is your season and cannot be denied except by the Lord which has given you that season. A leader knows his limitation is really not a limitation, but more so a direct obstacle of caution. Your life should be filled with many attempts to accomplish an abundance of specific projects to serve the Lord our God. Prepare for your season as you would prepare for your earnings. Wait on your season as if you have already received your season and the multiplying of your season will be a harvest of joy.

Anything that you set out to accomplish is only a great work of honesty away. You cannot be denied what has been promised to you. That which you have been given cannot be taken by the hands that are not worthy. There is no man that can withhold your season once it has been pronounced. Enjoin in the coming forth of all that is promised to you and bear witness to your season, as humbleness and humility will be about you. Concentrate on moving mountains with the faith of a mustard seed. Meditate daily on building your inner spirit as you would in troubled days. Pray for strength and operate as though you have the power of a thousand men. Let your attitude reflect righteous and wise men, who sit in counsel and investigate the nourishment of the gifts of life. Precious is the leader's breaths as he walks daily in the light without shivering in the face of the enemy. Stand strong and know that your season is in and you shall prevail in all that you endeavor. And when all has been lived, it is then that your season has arrived.

THE RULE 2:22 PRINCIPLE

(OLD TESTAMENT)

THE RULE 2:22 PRINCIPLE

(CHAPTER EIGHT)

DON'T DESTROY THOSE COMING FOR DELIVERANCE

DON'T DESTROY THOSE COMING FOR DELIVERANCE

This comes to be a great trial of many leaders whether male or female. You can find yourself at the top of the totem pole and have people continuously coming to serve God or even fulfill a purpose and mislead them due to your own self-centered egotistical plights. This subject becomes tough to digest for many of churchgoers because it often finds light being shed upon those leaders of the church that prey upon sheep assembling to serve God. This misuse of positions will surely have a consequence. To continue to flourish in the Lord's world, one must continue to keep all of His commandments. Do not mislead nor prey upon those that gather to serve the Lord. Do not lead them further away from a relationship with God, because they come with salivating hearts desiring the Lord.

Grieving Souls Become Easy Targets

For those of us that think that worldly things do not
find a place inside the church, I'm here to enlighten you
to sin. Just hearing the word sin calls people to
attention. We don't like to hear the word sin nowadays
because it points out wicked behavior among those
claiming to be servants of the Lord. The word sin is
often not even brought up in some congregations due to
a need for man to fulfill his own purpose through
deception. I challenge even those that have been
victimized by those that are in leadership and leading
souls to salvation. I issue the challenge because not all
are free from the blame because even though you
initially come for God, you fall for man. You fall to
your own self-deception of thinking the closer you get
to the man or men the closer or better off you are with
God. This has become a tremendous snag in churches
all over the world. Congregations are being insulted by

those leaders that feed them other than God's inspired word of the Gospel and fall for man's crafty misguidance.

1 Samuel 2:22 Now Eli was very old, and heard all that his sons did unto all Israel; and how they lay with the women that assembled at the door of the tabernacle of the congregation.

The door of the tabernacle was filled with women coming to serve the Lord. Eli's sons knew that these women were in need of a relationship and seeking to serve the Lord, but they misguided and even misused these women. We could spend tremendous amounts of time discussing various ways this was done or could be done however I wish to speak to the attitude and character of the men that practice this ungodly behavior. This behavior is intrusive and offensive against our Lord and Savior Jesus Christ. This willful sinning is appalling to the Lord. Souls are in need of

Jesus and man abandons his post in order to fulfill his lusts. In fulfilling his lustful intensions, he cripples the individual and the congregation from being able to move forward. Eli's sons' behavior was very offensive to their father and God because they were placed in a position of a shepherd or protection at the very least. Eli recognized that not only did his sons pervert themselves, they also hindered others from being able to submit themselves to the Lord.

This rule can also be initiated into all businesses and workplaces. The women addressed in this verse represent the character of people in need. Those of us that have ever had a single need have even gone through high waters to acquire that which we needed. Some of us have even found ourselves in uncompromising situations because along the way we lost track of our needs and followed our lusts. This doesn't mean just a sexual lust but it also encompasses material lust. Maybe we saw a way to raise ourselves up to a certain standard by our own rules and we abandoned having faith in God to fulfill our needs. We quickly waiver in faith and therefore even though we turn to God in mind, we turn from God through seeking to fulfill the desires of the flesh.

I've seen and heard women express how fond they are to men in leadership that appear to have their life altogether and I've also seen where those same women have been misled and abused because they lost sight of what they were actually there to do. Now those in power have taken the privilege that God has given them and misused their positioning to seduce the hearts of these women. We have to be careful of the games we play in the Lord's kingdom. We have to be careful and know that sin lurks even within the branches of Zion that cover the face of the earth. No one is without sin and what that does is let us know that we all need to have total faith in God because we can't manage ourselves on our own and stay the course of righteousness. Any man who thinks high of himself believing he is above this and doesn't need God will surely crumble.

I can't tell you that there doesn't arise a feeling of admiration for those with the light of the Lord over them, but I can tell you that those with the light of the Lord over their lives have a greater responsibility for themselves and those under their leadership. Souls that have been abused and used for all sorts of sinful fulfillment pour into churches seeking the one and only true healing of Jesus. They must not be preyed upon as filthy gain. God desires for us to be blessed and receive his rewards of obedience to His Word. For the most part, we have all heard the loose scriptural reciting. "To whom much is given, much is required!" These words appearing short in phrase pack a very strong punch.

These very same words find pastors, preachers, deacons, and even deaconess placed in a position where the physical contact they have with those seeking the Lord can easily affect the relationship of man-to-man but man-to-God.

Deceit Disguised as Divinity

I know personally of women that have been spoken to in a seductive manner by pastors but just enough that the pastor can hide behind the fulfillment of a scriptural duty or guidance. Pastors and other men have held the hands of women and prayed with them as a means of fulfilling their lusts for women as well as inappropriately caressing the body of women while displaying a caught in the spirit moment. Now this is tough to discuss without causing a panic but I'm leaning on the Lord to awaken us to a rule that should not be neglected for it is hurting those already hurt much deeper than what we see surface level. Eli's sons used their positions and the women's position and posture at the door of the tabernacle as a means to fulfill their lusts. One can argue on whether they came intentionally to carry out their worldly ways at the outset but we know one thing for sure, they violated not only God's trust, but they violated the trust of their father, and the trust of the women that assembled at the door of the tabernacle.

Men should find themselves in an honored position of God having placed you on the earth to provide protection over women and children and most importantly to carry out your obedience to Him. Maybe, and just maybe if we would see ourselves being harmed by the actions of other men then we would change our ways. If we could imagine at the time of our sins, what if this was my wife , my daughter, my mother, or any woman close to us we would not hurt those that need our protection and God's deliverance. If leaders would grab hold of this rule and hold our pastor friends, preacher friends, deacon friends, and men as a whole accountable for their actions then we could help put an end to this corruption that overtakes the congregation. When one person is offended by these ungodly actions then we should all be offended. We have to crack open a very noticeable hole in these carnal circles of church leaders that flock together, chase women, and share stories of how they have sinned with members of their congregations. Do not think because leaders share their sins with you that it makes it okay for you to continue your sinning, nor does it help your situation. You should not attach yourselves to those that corroborate your sins and encourage you down the wrong path. We have to help our brothers and expose their harmful sins against people. We will stand in encouragement of corrected behavior but we will not become a part of hurting already hurt people. We will call them back to the path of the obedience of God. We must become the faithful priest raised by God to correct the wrong of men and carryout God's order. For those that live as Eli's sons did, God tell us in verse *31 Behold, the days come, that I will cut off thine arm, and the arm of thy father's house, that there shall not be an old man in thine home.* We clearly see that our now behavior will hinder our sons and their sons' houses.

THE RULE 2:22 PRINCIPLE

(CHAPTER NINE)

FOLLOW THROUGH WHEN GOD ANOINTS YOU

FOLLOW THROUGH WHEN GOD ANOINTS
YOU

The greatest mistake we can make often times when God has anointed us to be placed in a certain position is yield to the enemy's counter-move of placing someone else before us. This can be the move that's underscored by a leader overlooking you or trying to keep you from reaching your destiny chosen by God. You know you've been anointed the successor of the present leadership however the powers that be have plans to hinder your advancement and God's plans. Those of us not desiring to cause a ruckus or upset the perceived order will just fall in line with the deception placed before us. Most likely, we are even pressured by those around us to just go along with the program because of the apparent leadership that controls their every move and thought. Be careful that you do not subject yourselves to leadership for which God has raised you up to lead. Your faith in God is what should command you to standfast and obey the Word of God. Yes, "the steps of a righteous man are ordered by God." It can be quite disturbing and lonely when everyone around you and your leadership sees the hand of the Lord upon your life, but all the same no one wishes to see you take your rightful position. What should you do? Should you bow down and fall in line with man or stand in the authority of God and take your rightful position? You should not hesitate in obeying God's Word. As surely as God has anointed you, He has also properly prepared you with all that you will ever need to fulfill that which is needed for your office.

Opposition Will Strike

2 Samuel 2: 22 So Abner said again to Asahel, "Turn aside from following me. Why should I strike you to the ground? How then could I face your brother

Joab? Abner, the captain of Saul's army was very aware of David's anointing to be the king as Saul has died. Using the power of his position as captain, Abner went against God's apparent anointing of David as king and chose Ishboseth, Saul's son, to be king. The challenge to us as the anointed is to walk in the strength of God and know that there will be opposition that dwells upon our path of destiny, but we cannot align ourselves with those that oppose God's order regardless of the positions they hold. Our anointing has nothing to do with us and everything to do with God's plan. When we fail to operate in the manner in which God has anointed us to do, then we not only affect our advancement but the advancement of all those around us and those to come.

Abner provoking Joab to what he thinks is a genius plan to further disrupt David's army and kingship, requests that the men of both army's face-off and battle.

Here we find that twelve of Abner's men and twelve of David's men face-off in battle and they thrust swords into each other's sides. This day however, Abner was defeated. As the story goes on, Abner was pursued by others and killed few while David's army killed many of Abner's army.

What we should learn from this is the fact that the anointing on our lives does not mean that we will not incur hardships or injuries but God's anointing assures us of the victory. When times are tough, we press on. When times seemingly are complex and have no resolution, we press on. When times are arguably the worst we've seen, we press on for God is victorious in our favor. Never forget that you are anointed to do the work of the Lord and not the work of yourselves. When we take our eyes off the aim of God, we forego circumspectly thinking, bringing about a discourse to our destination.

Behind the Secret Anointing

When you walk in the presence of the Lord do not be surprised that the people around you are not surprised that God has favored you. This was David's position. David had inquired of the Lord. After David's inquiring of the Lord, it was obvious to everyone and all of Israel's enemies that David would become king. After consulting the Lord, the men of Judah came to anoint David king over the house of Judah.

God has already set you up for leadership before you were anointed. God has already prepared your troops. God has already solidified your ranks. Just remember that God has done this for you, so you do not have to search for what God has already given you. When we're searching for what we think we need, instead of receiving what God has already given us, we end up causing destruction to our ranks. Under David's anointing over the house of Judah, the city of Hebron would prove to be a resource as other tribes would align themselves to David.

Here's the key you may have missed in all of this. The public anointing was exactly as it was, a public affair. The men of David were the first to witness his private anointing, as well as publicly and openly acknowledging the anointing. What God has for you, will not always be done out in public.

God is the best of planners. He is the Master of creativity. He is the author of the greatest strategies ever. All we have to do is beckon unto his commandments and obey his voice. There are no complications when God has prepared the way. What we claim as complications are our unwillingness to face the trials and tribulations that come our way. We set ourselves to believe that we will not face any opposition or pressure when He has promised us victory. God has already provided the victory but we still have to fight the battle.

The worldly thought is that we may win the battle but lose the war, but with God, we secure the battle and God has already seized the war in His favor. Our job is not to fight the war, but to fight the good fight. It is in God's wisdom that the war is won. Our individual and collective battles are segments of a bigger picture that God has perfected through man's imperfections. Our focus on winning a war sidetracks us and ensures that we see ourselves as failures when we engage certain battles that don't seem to end in the best for us.

Sometimes when we think that we have lose a battle, time passes quite a bit before we realize that we actually won the battle. Your removal from a certain job, a certain office, a certain person, a certain situation, or a certain spirit is God's grace over your life to keep you from future harm. As carnal mindsets seek to overcome the spirit, we crash and burn thinking only of

the moment not even realizing we've been under God's

wings of protection from the outset. This is why you

must "follow through when God anoints you."

THE RULE 2:22 PRINCIPLE

(CHAPTER TEN)

ISSUE THE PITCHING ORDER

ISSUE THE PITCHING ORDER

Everyone that comes into your camp should pitch by your orders. Details of discipline are a must. Don't confuse this with micro-managing your people. Don't confuse this with micro-managing however manage through the eye of a microscope to ensure you understand the heartbeat of your people and the pulse of their lives. Ideally, we align ourselves to the teacher that reflects an opinion of thought that we have surrendered to in order to build upon like values. That's not a bad practice however it limits most people because they abandon their own dreams and visions for the sake of living out their leader's dreams and visions by way of indirect force.

Being a great leader starts with being a great follower. You can organize your leadership in the midst of your days of following. When you become the leader, you're pitching follows the methodology of

225

understanding the follower who is self-sufficient enough to understand that leadership is learning to first follow with authority. Pitching by your design will become normal once your followers submit themselves to the greater authority, which is God. Your people must understand that you are also teaching them to pitch by the Creator of all pitching orders. Once they understand that, then you can effectively conquer all that you set out to acquire.

Teach Them How to Pitch

The leader you aim to be is one that teaches them to pitch by your orders. Pitching by your order aligns your people, ranks your people, fills the gaps between your people, and teaches them to trust your people. You will not have to focus on loyalty if you issue the pitching order. Most camps, groups, squads, or teams only focus on loyalty before placing their people in ranks. Where is the real strength if we as leaders only focus on loyalty first? Loyalty does not all the time equal relationship. Loyalty usually comes with a test presented by a leader that shames or takes away from the real character of a person in order to blackmail or establish proof that one will hold true to an oath.

Issuing the pitching order provides you with clarity of where each person of the ranks is as it relates to their stability. This means you build a personal relationship with them. *Numbers 2:22 Then the tribe of Benjamin; and the captain of the sons of Benjamin shall be Abidan the son of Gideoni.* We find that at the outset, the Lord had spoken unto Moses approximately eighty-five times throughout the Book of Numbers. Here we can gather that the one issuing the pitching order must hear from God and not man. The details by which we pitch our lives encompass business, church, home, and school to be in high priority.

Moses was to pay strict attention that the people were freshly released from the slavery of Egypt. Those people that come under your leadership will need pitching orders as they are still yoked to old leadership although they have found refuge in your camp. The tabernacle of your camp or the meeting place of your camp should be the focal place where all your people should be developed. By the time the orders of ranking reach the tribe of Benjamin in verse 22 of Numbers chapter 2, a great pitching order has been established that can be traced back to the pitching order of Moses. What this assures you, as the leader, is that you can venture into any squad or rank and find the head of the camp's mirrored ranking without having to wonder if they've received certain details.

Often times we take the mindset of "need-to-know" basis so strictly that those that fall into the ranking begin to withhold that which you have not designed to be withheld. By the time the pitching order reaches the lower ranks your forces have been weakened. Leaders need to be well acquainted with the heartbeat of their people and the pulse of their lives. Of course as your numbers grow, you will assign leaders under you to establish relationship but you must never become detached from your people because after all they are your people. They will trust you and give you loyalty if you properly build a relationship with them through your designated leaders as long as they know they have a relationship that is trustworthy enough that they can honestly say they know you and you know them.

Know Where to Pitch

Where will you train your people to pitch? You cannot train your leaders in one camp and then train your people in another camp. In other words, your people must receive the exact training you give your leaders. The focal point of your camp is the tabernacle of your camp and not the situation of your camp. The world will overshadow the tabernacle if your people see that you are disconnected due to your leaders teaching them to pitch about worldly aims.

Leaders must tap into the focal point of their camps and feed each and every person from the same feeding tube. Leaders you assign to people sometimes become distracted by their positions and titles that they begin to poison the feeding tubes of your people to become closer to you or fear their people will build a closer relationship to you than they have. Will you support your leaders' corrupt actions over their subordinates or will you stand for justice showing all of your people that there is no separation amongst them? This is where most leaders lose their power and relationship with their camp and their dominion begins to decline. The worse thing a leader can do at this point is be in denial that they may have assigned an overly zealous leader to their people. The real leader must see himself as one with the slain lamb spoken of in Revelation 5:6 in the midst of the throne and of the four beasts and in the midst of the elders. A true friend (leader) will have about himself the loyalty of self-sacrifice and self-abnegation.

The perfect plan for pitching can only be issued by the leader that is inspired by godly principles of pitching that he will use to affect his people throughout his camp. The pitching order is one that cannot and must not be deterred from for any reason. Where we loosely say everything is not in black and white, I beg to differ to tell you that there must not be any grey areas in issuing the pitching orders. The moment you leave room for grey, this will be the moment you begin to surrender your camp to the enemy. The leader must be affixed to the focal point of the camp and nurture not only the physical focus but the spiritual focus, which is

priority.

THE RULE 2:22 PRINCIPLE

(CHAPTER ELEVEN)

KEEP GLEANING IN YOUR FIELD

KEEP GLEANING IN YOUR FIELD

In the realm of entrepreneurialism, we run from one project to another without protection of our sanity or God's guidance. It would be fair to say that we spread ourselves thin and we abandon our ideas in lieu of other things that capture our attention. One of the worst things we can do in the pursuit of success in any venture we set our hearts towards, is stop working in our field to go work in someone else's field.

Often times this leaves you uncovered and unaligned to certain principles that were designed to give you knowledge through experience. When you settle to focus on what someone else says will make you successful then you cannot prove to yourself that you maintain the purity of your vision. Your vision will become the life of those you choose to follow instead of those you set out to lead. Your field of play and work are uniquely yours and it is up to you to put your hand to the plow and cultivate your field. Your field is your design board, arena, mirror, and graphing paper to plot all your entrepreneurial sets. Your field is awaiting you to subdue it with unyielding faith.

Don't Jump Ship

Ruth 2:22 And Naomi said to Ruth her daughter-in-law, "It is good, my daughter, that you go out with his young women, and that people do not meet you in another field." I've discussed a similar principle in my previous work, "Follow the Leader (Resurrecting Men to Leadership)." I also stated principles of "Put All Your Eggs in One Basket" and "You Don't Need a B Plan." Here I wish to develop the Rule 2:22 principle giving you the understanding that too often we set out in a particular venture we believe will bring us a level of success and we abandon our dreams because we see that someone else's field has produced a certain success. Jumping ship or hopping on the bandwagon is often associated with being fans of a particular sports team or maybe a general idea.

Many successful people have been known to become successful because despite the years of setback in attempting to become successful through working their dreams, they stay persistent. Commitment and consistency were their best attributes for success. All you have to do is research Oprah Winfrey, Tyler Perry, or even Bill Gates. These notable persons all stayed the course. Despite the setbacks, the opinions of people, or the personal torturing they inflicted upon themselves they stayed in their field and became the recipient of reaping what was sewn. As Tyler Perry would put it and I must say I love that he acknowledges the real truth of it all, "It was the grace of God which ultimately afforded him the opportunity to be as great and successful as he is."

This resembles a particular major in college. A million people a year attend college majoring in Business Administration or Business Management however those same people will never work the world's field to bring about great harvest. They will only glean in the businesses of others without setting out to glean in a field trusting God that their labor will manifest their own corporations. These same college graduates will abandon their fields and settle to work in areas where they will nerve exercise their acquired knowledge.

Glean Until You Can't Glean

Chapter two of Ruth displays Ruth placed in a field where she would be protected while she worked. To understand this more, we must acknowledge that Ruth was already working before she was assured protection. Many of us have great ideas but we seek for others to give us a level of protection before we begin to work our visions. This protection comes in the form of some desired approval of your vision, financing of your vision, or celebration of your vision. I want to tell you that if continue to wait on any of these before you commence to work your vision then you have already failed. You should not expect for anyone to see the totality of the vision that God gives you and support it in totality. In fact, you can probably expect plenty of opposition verbally and silently. This may even come by way of exposing your vision to those with shallow vision. Your family is not always the best people to expose a great vision to. You know your family better than anyone else. You know their mentality whether it by envy, greed, or jealousy. This doesn't mean that your entire family will not be supportive. Support even given in prayer is a strong advantage point that businesses can thrive from.

Ruth gleaned from the harvest of successful produce. What does this mean for you? This means that you are to remain in your field and not wonder off into other fields. Ruth started out gleaning from the grain left behind after the harvesters had worked through the grain fields collecting produce but as a result of her diligence of protecting her mother-in-law and working in the field, she received more. Boaz placed her amongst the harvesters and gave the harvesters an order to leave great produce behind for her to glean from. Had Ruth left the field in which she initially set out to work, she would have missed the blessing. Also, in addition to missing the blessing, Ruth would have removed herself from under the umbrella of protection she was allowed to glean. God watches how faithful we are over little things before he gives us the master role over many. We may think that we would do well managing a larger amount but if we can't work

diligently in small numbers then there's no way we can
control larger or promotion from God.

The Season to Glean

Never underestimate the reason that you have to stay
in your field and not abandon it for another, is because
the seasons continuously evolve and revolve at God's
command. The seasons bring about certain crops in
certain fields. Ruth was privileged as she was in the
right field at the right time because she simply just went
to work in the field she looked into in order to live out
her vision. You must work your field each season as if
the harvest is plenty. You have to make the same
preparations time after time regardless of the condition
of the field. Despite how many people show up to your
shop, attend your business meeting, seek you out for
service, or become repeat customers, you have a duty to
plan, prepare, and produce as if you have pre-sold out

crowds or business ventures. This is the protection you are afforded when you stay in your field and work through the various seasons regardless of the harvest you glean.

Glean with expectation that your gleaning will multiply if you believe and trust God's ordered steps. Believe in what you plant and expect tremendous growth. Work as though you will never get the chance to glean in your vision ever again. Glean with the heart of helping others. Glean with a heart of a champion and do not be dismayed. Glean knowing you are privileged by God to be uniquely you in the field you choose to employ.

THE RULE 2:22 PRINCIPLE

(CHAPTER TWELVE)

KEEP THE WAY OF THE LORD

KEEP THE WAY OF THE LORD

The gods of this world shall be a snare to you in and about everywhere you turn. What you face in this world can be taken as a reminder to stay the course of God or hinder your destiny. Trendsetting has become a major crippler of the Gospel of Christ in today's time. It has become a trend to attempt to offset the Gospel with the nuances of the world. We as a people are misguided to watered-down views of the Gospel and fight for more liberality than strict obedience to the Word of God. We cannot serve this world and gain spiritual prosperity merely praying to God as he does not reign supreme. It is of utmost importance that we keep the way of the Lord and follow not the way of the gods of this world. The gods of this world are adultery, fornication, homosexuality, murder, theft, vanity, and an overwhelming spirit of chasing financial prosperity for personal gain. Reality is foregone in lieu of television

243

living. What we deem as reality has now overridden the presence of God. We cannot fail to uphold our morals and values of God in order to pursue the world. We can have material gain without abandoning our spiritual guidance if only we persevere to endure with patience. We can never be denied for that which God has for us. Despite what the world tells us, you can adhere to your spirituality and become successful without selling out to worldly principles that contradict the presence of God in our lives. There must be an undeniable determination to maintain obedience in keeping ourselves aligned to God's word. This is the finishing testimony God wishes for us to display to the world.

Be Careful Who and What You Serve

If you really want to find out where your heart is, just look where you donate and spend the most money. Hobbies can be relaxing but it can also become your god if you're not careful. We self- indulge in things that will get us no closer to the Kingdom of God but bring us worldly recognition. We have become obsessed with the various forms of social media and it's no particular one I wish to identify. All forms of social media have become the gods of our time. Social media has demonized our time that should be spent building a closer relationship with God. You have to ask yourself how much time do I spend a week on the social media sites. Be all inclusive, because this could even mean you spend too much time on social media in the promotion of your businesses. God addresses the snares that will overtake us in Judges Chapter 2. He simply tells us that he will not dismiss them from amongst us and they will be a thorn in our side. Self-control is propelled to the front of many things that we need to have for spiritual prosperity and to ensure ourselves we do not follow the false gods. *Judges 2: 22 That through them I may prove Israel, whether they will keep the way*

of the Lord to walk there in, as their fathers did keep it,

or not.

Be the Judge amongst the People

Repentance should be a part of our daily lives. Repentance should come as much as we breathe. God raised up judges amongst the repented people for them to be delivered back to the way of the Lord. Each and every believer of Christ should consider himself or herself a judge appointed by God to deliver the people out of the hands of the enemy back to the way of the Lord. Christians provide justice in the understanding of the Hebrew word *shopet*. To the liking of the judge that sits upon the courthouse bench, a judge gives an order or ordinance for the verdict of the guilty to be carried out in that the guilty should be punished and set-a-straight of the law.

The judgment spoken of here is to bring about the justice of God in returning His people back to His way. We cannot justifiably let people serve gods other than our Lord and Savior Jesus Christ without sharing the Gospel of Christ with them. Many Christians have faltered in aligning themselves with workforce guidelines that state that religion cannot be discussed at their places of employment. However there is freedom in desecrating the work environment with sexually perverse jokes and videos with no punishment to be delivered. We as believers are asked to mask our religious morals and values as not to offend people of other religions. The scriptures do not agree with this concept of being politically correct. This does not mean that we are to brutally attack others of different beliefs than ours.

Our society has bowed out of serving Christ to serve the god of Baalim. Baal indicated as the fertility god of the Canaanites was viewed to bring about the productivity of crops, animals, and men. Additionally, Baal was also considered a god of the weather. Elijah denied Baal and took him to trial upholding God in the presence of Baal's supposed title as "god of the fire." Sadly, we find many of people upholding man as God due to a position or title. Just maybe that leader has predicted some already calculated occurrences that amazed the unlearned of the Gospel.

Recognize Apostasy

Apostasy has become so inflamed these days because most of us would believe that we still follow God as we give more attention to the physically present beings and are without the visual presence of God. There is an overlooking of Hebrews 11:1 which tells us that faith is the substance of things hoped for (not yet seen). We turn our attentions to even the crosses we wear around our necks as if they carry some range of power. We lose track that the ornaments only serve as a reminder of God and hold no spiritual or physical power. We serve the god of financial prosperity by affixing ourselves and our beliefs to organizations that bring about some worldly connectivity that affords us avenues of success. We easily commit apostasy in this manner but we would diligently argue that we still love God. Stating we love God is not serving God. When we don't serve God then we serve other gods of this world and fall into apostasy.

Religious tenets that embrace part but not the whole of the doctrine of Jesus Christ are forms of apostasy that bring great snares to believers who lack knowledge of the true doctrine of Christ. There must be a concerned re-evaluation of what apostasy looks like and how easy it is to commit apostasy without verbally saying you have turned from God. When we depend of the identities of other beings, forces, procedures, etc. to bless us then we have turned from God. The presence of the angel of the Lord must be felt in society to call God's people back to the way of the Lord. Judges must keep the way of the Lord and not bow to the lifestyles of the masses.

THE RULE 2:22 PRINCIPLE

(CHAPTER THIRTEEN)

PRESERVE GOD'S PROVIDENCE

PRESERVE GOD'S PROVIDENCE

Society's idea of success has taken on Pharaoh's charge to bring about an execution of all males, as they forego their intellectual and inventive nature in pursuit of crippling crossovers, wicked jump shots, blitzing hits and rumbling receptions aiming to hold score at the end zone, realizing they are the end of the zone. Skilled orators and speakers of humanity's platform have traded in their lively liberations of spoken word to elevate our people in hopes of being the next hot rapper. As these fields are filled with intelligent individuals, the killing fields are not only the streets but an industry aimed at killing the minds of future leaders that will usher society back to the spiritual essence of what man was created to be. Man needs an exit strategy for all the brilliant minds that carry the football, shoot the basketball, and grace the microphones exposing their gifts so that Pharaoh's plot strives to live out his rule. *Exodus 2:22 And Pharaoh charged all his people, saying, Every son that is born ye shall cast into the river, and every daughter ye shall save alive.*

So it is that the age old complaint that we often hear is that all good men are either dead, gay, or in jail. To fall into this fictional thinking is to not believe in God's providence. God has universally caused Pharaoh's plan to fail. Leaders preserve God's providence by ensuring that we do not leave behind our brothers that are gay or incarcerated and we honor the spirit of life which our deceased brothers have left behind by being good stewards of humanity. Each trial that mankind faces subjects man, woman and child to a life of disorder propagated by society's hints of discourse. Adhering to the exit strategy that we train our men to lead spiritually before they can lead physically, we not only prepare them for the annals of a disastrous world but we prepare them for the resurrection of male leadership. Properly

253

positioned, the birth of every male should be seen as Moses and each male's life is one that can and shall lead God's people to the Promise Land. No matter where we find our men tossed in the river, we know that their deliverance will be unto a priestly tribe where their appearance shall be the indication of healthy and vigorous conditioning. It takes a village to raise a child and therefore we find that our females are also subjected to Pharaoh's demands. As worldly intervention seeps through the gaps of spiritual bonding, females are forced to take on the males' role which indirectly places them at the pits of catastrophe in seeking empathy and sympathy from another female attempting to fulfill a man's role.

Provide the Protection

Preserving God's providence ensures us that we shall follow the design of each-one-teach-one and not fall into the complacency of envy, hate, and jealousy of the next human being. As Pharaoh had widened his charge to kill all males, there is an onslaught of attacks aimed at males regardless of color, creed, race, nationality, etc. We have a duty to protect the birth rights of our males, keeping them in hiding to preserve our existence. Keeping them in hiding is to secure them from any and all activities that threaten their calling and purpose. The strengthening of young males shall be matured by strong fathers. Fathers are subject to godly leadership in their marriages and homes. Even greater than the family and home limits, fathers have a duty to represent our communities and society as a whole to prevent Pharaoh's attack upon our nation. Scripture tells us in *Ephesians 6:12 For we wrestle not against flesh and blood, but against principalities, against powers, against the rulers of the darkness of this world, against spiritual wickedness in high places.*

This is the mindset we as people must understand about the true nature of the fight being spiritual and not carnal. The enemies we face are the spirits and not the people we become dissatisfied with because of their actions or presence. We offer up intercession and prayer for those incapable of defending themselves against the principalities. Pharaoh's charge becomes void when we fulfill the will of God to be our brother's keeper. A preservation of life and diligence driven towards our destinies shall be prevalent and prioritized amongst worldly affixations.

Make a Strong Presence

There has to be a strong presence of male leadership in the world today. There must be a presence that is seen, heard, and actively martyring. Fathers are needed to father their sons and love and raise their daughters to know what to look for in a man. Fathers need to be well-rounded examples of a man to their sons. Men must teach honor of a woman and love and respect should be shown to our women. Chivalry is not dead and man should promote more of it.

Pharaoh's charge has no dominion over man. Man was created with a God purpose and divine calling on his life to subdue this earth. That shall be the grounds on which we preserve God's providence. Our birth shall not be in vain. We will receive proper training at home and then teach the world. We will not subject ourselves to the worldly was of Pharaoh's ideas. Our abilities shall be encouraged, exhorted, and uplifted throughout the days of our lives. We will stand in the gap for every male that is born and not be turned from them due to the principalities that plague us all. We will fight the spirits that come against us with the power and authority of God. We will not sit down with fear in our hearts but we shall unite and fight the good fight. We shall press on towards the mark of our higher calling in the name of Jesus. The streets shall not have our sons as they are the raging waters held back by God in which Pharaoh's army was drowned. God is forever present and we worship not this world but He who created this world. The rivers that run wild shall not hold the bodies of our males for they shall receive the protection and upbringing from priestly families. Our exit strategy shall be in the Lord our God. We will not substitute God for worldly solutions.

THE RULE 2:22 PRINCIPLE

(CHAPTER FOURTEEN)

TAKE POSSESSION OF REJECTED PROPOSALS

TAKE POSSESSION OF REJECTED PROPOSALS

We come to the table with peace. We pray for peace. We seek to bring about order and submit ourselves to serve in peace but our proposals become rejected from intimidation. Take possession of rejected proposals. We go the limit to preserve peace but there are always signs of demonic intervention reckoning the physicality of people producing spiritual wickedness.

This rule speaks to serving in peace and being attacked in wickedness. God has given you the spirit of humbleness and now God desires for you to take possession of the rejected proposals. Hostile rebuking has come your way too many times and you've acted in peace but your territory is going to be expanded as the tables must be turned. This is called being privileged and rewarded for your stewardship. You partner in prayer to overcome the enemy. Your territory is already being expanded because intimidation strikes that fear in your enemy where they can't stand still because they see your popularity increasing. You must come from under the hostile leadership and strike out on your own and heed the words of God. Your season for following is up and God has propelled you into leadership to replace those that have been disobedient to the voice of God. *Deuteronomy 2:22 Rise ye up, take the journey, and pass over the river Arnon: behold, I have given into thine hand Sihon the Amorite, the king of Heshbon, and his land: begin to possess it, and contend with him in battle.*

Immediately Follow the Order

Israel was given the order not to fight the tribes of Edom, Moab, and Ammon however this was not the case as it came to Sihon, the Amorite. Israel had received a change of order. Sihon received words of peace from messengers of Moses and he rejected them.

In the end, God's observance of the circumstances surrounding Sihon brought about an issuance to completely destroy Sihon and his people.

We obey God's words of peace however the time comes when God tells us to take to territory and destroy the leader and his people. What does this mean? Does this mean kill the leader and kill his people? This is a symbolic overtaking. Destroy it all. God has placed you in the arena to correct the wickedness that has come about in the land. Leaders fall into the realm of worshipping themselves and forgetting God. In the same manner, their people begin to worship the leader instead of God without any correction. God has centered and covered you to take the territory. God builds your favor, your popularity, your strength, and your takeover. Now you don't have to remain in the wicked kingdom in order to overtake it. God will prepare you to overtake it by taking from it as the wicked declines in power. Do not be confused that it is you that secures the battle but God does use you to maneuver through the battle.

When God begins to use you to destroy the wicked heads of leadership you do not negotiate unto the enemy's surrender. You do not negotiate another peace treaty. You do not initiate a cease fire. You destroy the leader and the people. God intends to destroy and replenish the kingdom of wickedness with righteous leadership. God's structure sometimes seems harsh but we must remember that the flames of the hell fire are harshly heated. We do not serve in lukewarm status. We serve in such a capacity that reflects obedience of God. We must be stern in understanding and carrying out the order of God to destroy the wickedness that surrounds us. Your work environments, pleasure places, circles of friendship, and even your family arenas are all touched by the principalities of Satan. God tells us to stand tall and destroy those leaders and their people that corrupt the atmosphere of God. Here's the test that we so often fail. We cower down to those that are close to us and walk out on God sparing those wicked spirits to continue in ungodly manners. If you ever intend to press toward the mark of the higher calling you will first need to be obedient to God and press forward through the yokes of family and friends that criticize you for following God's orders.

The Peace Treaty is over

The aim here is to establish or resurrect the burden of proof that Christ will stand for us as He has commanded us to stand for him. The peace treaty is over and not relevant for this time or this people. The command has been given to destroy everything in sight and trust God's plan for them and you. Don't focus on the ability of the enemy just focus on the strength of

God. Surely when God has issued you the orders to destroy, He has properly prepared you for victory. Essentially, you are not fighting the battle it is God fighting the battle for you.

Your journey shall be filled with fight but your destiny will be filled with promise. Don't die in your hesitation to follow the orders of God. Those around you may or will question your motives but when you surround yourself with others in godly relationships, you will have the support you need. Just as much as you, they will be eager to fight in the cause of God. When you say go they will react without hesitation because the order they hear will come from you but the spirit of the order will be felt from God. Taking possession of rejected proposals is the reality of God's promise that His word shall not return unto him void. This is martyring for the Lord. God's work cannot be judged by man and should not be held up by man's questioning of God's work. When God gives you orders to destroy certain territory, you strap on the entire armor of God and you destroy everything insight and the people. You don't leave the people because they will carry on the old leader's ideas. They will reestablish corrupt territory that God did not intend to be left. Take possession of rejected proposals because God is giving you expansion.

THE RULE 2:22 PRINCIPLE

(CHAPTER FIFTEEN)

UTLIZE THE RIB

UTILIZE THE RIB

At mankind's inception of being God's greatest creation, he was brought into the world with completion. This outlines the start of processing who we are from birth and what was instilled in us for living out successful lives far beyond the thoughts of financial wealth. Spiritual growth will prepare you for material growth. As we find in the Holy Bible, *Genesis 2:22 And the rib, which the Lord God had taken from man, made he a woman, and brought her unto the man.* Here is the first time in the history of creation that God had spoken and said something was *not good.* God's hands sterilized and prepared for surgery, put man under spiritual anesthesia to bring out of man, that which would not only give him spiritual completion but physical completion.

The limitation of man's intellect was unknown to all from the beginning of time as God paraded all the species of the earth in front of man and they received names. Without having to research, call someone, conduct any type of investigation, man was endowed with spiritual revelation from God to perform in the likeness of God because he was not controlled by his environment, but he exercised dominion over the environment. The rib here represents the spiritual essence man was born with and how we seem to forget that all of what we need is already inside of us. The miraculous supernatural agency of this divine surgery causes us to reflect upon woman being brought forth to be a help meet to man. Woman is representative of that which was in man and man's inability to bring forth all of that which God created in him. Woman as the rib had to be brought forth from man, by God, to exercise a physical completion that man would need to complete the commands of God through being fruitful, replenishing, and subduing the earth.

Men Persevering Over Life's Obstacles

The challenge man faces on a daily basis is that we fail to utilize the rib. In part and whole, we speak to the aspect of the rib spiritually and physically. Men persevering over life's obstacles (M'P.O.L.O.) has taken man's focus from living out his purpose and walking in his calling. When man focuses on the problems of the world, he leans to the forces of battle through worldly means and completely disregards or neglects the rib. The rib being the problem solving agent instilled deep within man's intellect giving him opportunity to exercise his God likeness of moral and natural character, is forsaken or obsolete at this point. Causing a mental combustion of psychological probing, the rib lays dormant within man, as a new tool in a toolbox, opting to utilize a pair of pliers for a metric wrench job. So where man can grip the problem, he latches on but continues to slip and create an even greater problem by forgoing the use of the rib that lies within his spiritual and physical toolbox.

The rib in its Hebrew form is *tslea'* meaning "side," "wing of a building," or a "panel" indicated throughout the Old Testament sheds light upon an area of man that he can withdraw a resource. Too often man seeks to withdraw resources stored within someone else instead of himself. Man settles upon the practices of the world and not his creative likeness or nature. Man was created with giftedness. As woman or the rib was being brought forth to balance the life of man's necessities, God had planned for man to conquer all that he would face giving him equal ability to overcome any problem he would face. Labeled as a help meet, the rib or woman, balances a man's physical nature that he be completed as that which was in him has now become manifested into a physical existence that he can see. This fault of man is a symbolism to man's lack of confidence in who he really is and whom he was created in the image of. It is not until man sees a physical representation of God that man gathers up the strength to exercise that which has already been in him. The woman gives the man comfort, confidence, a place of retreat, healthy and spiritual nurturing of his ego and the support that she believes in him to do just what he was called to do by God. She, the rib, protects the vital organ of her king as he now musters up the fortitude to command and demand all matters of the world to become subjected to his dominion.

Exercise Your Likeness to God

In order to utilize the rib, man is forced to investigate his conscience which will supplement his will to listen to the voice of God. Man should take heed that when God has commanded one to do something then he has already prepared him for the occasion.

Revisiting the command to "be fruitful, replenish, and subdue" the earth, man needs a wakeup call. God has planted the seed of entrepreneurship within the soul of man. God has planted the seed of production within the soul of man. God has planted the seed of cultivation within the soul of man. God has planted the seed of fertilization within the soul of man. God has planted the seed of fatherhood within the soul of man. God has planted the seed of completion within the soul of man. When man controls his environment with the intellect that God has given him from creation, there is no way he can walk the face of the earth doomed to ruin. It is ultimately impossible for a man exercising his likeness to God and affixed to the moral and natural characteristics of God to be destitute. Man's nature is to utilize the rib for that which he was born with, and it must be taken out of him and used for the advancement of humanity.

Man's presence and placement in the garden is symbolic that wherever man finds himself in this world placed by God, it is a place where God not only intends for him to work but has prepared him to work the harvest and lead the laborers into unity. The utilization of the rib is a greater mindset of the resources provided by the source of all things to be well within man's control when he utilizes the rib as the foundation principle of completion. Every need will therefore be met and provision for others shall also be afforded and instituted into humanity.

THE RULE 2:22 PRINCIPLE

(CHAPTER SIXTEEN)

WAIT UP IN THE MOUNTAINS

WAIT UP IN THE MOUTAINS

Begin your journey by fleeing to the mountains to observe the territory you are preparing to inherit. You have to prepare for greater by positioning yourself to become knowledgeable of the promise God is giving you. The entrepreneurial leader will seek out the land he intends to inherit long before he will seize it. This means preparing your mind to conquer territory for which you seek the Lord to subdue. Often times we seek to start businesses but we do little surveying. This little surveying may be a hinderance because we see job postings and notice the salary is exceptionally higher than what we are used to acquiring in our past employment. If you only rely on the posted description of the job vacancy then all you have done is aligned yourself with the adequate information that every other person is privileged to. The leader who prepares himself by researching in depth will become more than a novice at the entry level positioning.

Enabling yourself with prior knowledge of a corporation works to your benefit as you will be abreast company policies which you can generally find searching websites or talking with personnel employed at the particular corporation for which you wish to be employed. This may even be the research you need to conduct as you plan to begin a sole proprietorship. Do the homework. Get involved and do the intern's work of camping out in the mountains of the corporation in order to devise the takeover of your goals. Learn the inner workings of the entrepreneurial vision God has given you. Many visions become short lived because we never send out the spies to collect knowledge of the internal workings of the corporations. The spies I speak of are your intuitive characters that desire to know more about the craft. *Joshua 2:22 And they went, and came unto the mountain, and abode there three days, until the*

pursuers were returned: and the pursuers sought them

throughout all the way, but found them not.

The Territory Shall be Yours

Returning to chapter one of Joshua, we find that

Moses could not enter the Promise Land but it was a

must for Joshua. Joshua was armed with God's

commitment and promised the territory of wherever his

foot should tread upon. When God blesses you with the

calling and vision then the territory shall be yours

however there is still work for you to do. You cannot sit

back and judge your ability by the one that has led you

to a certain point. This also means that when God has

called you to a specific place, regardless of how great

your leader is or has been, you are destined for further

advancement by the will of God. Most times we limit

ourselves to that of our teacher's or trainer's ability and

we never know why they only reached as far as they have. We must also be careful not to let our leader's actions cripple our destinies that have been aligned by God, because our leader went as far as God saw fit. Our destiny is not about the thought of our leaders. We are in order of the leadership. We truly are in the order of God to follow the leadership for which we were placed as sheep but when God calls you to greater, you must answer the call regardless of who judges you. Your steps are ordered by God and not man. Your obedience to God's orders is for the advancement of the people that God has placed you to lead.

Verse 22 represents your positioning prior to overtaking the territory God has promised you. You must have mountain positioning. Why the mountain? In the mountain is representative of a place of high to enable you to observe the land for which you shall soon inherit. Three days represents the observation process and cover and concealment. You cannot plan to overtake a particular venture by dwelling in the ranks of the common people. Your thought process must be of those that are in the positions of leadership. Sheep only mingle in the herd and the shepherd leads the herd of sheep. If you have sheep mentality then you only operate within the limited territory where you are placed by the shepherd for protection. In this instance, leaders will emerge and jump the fence to expand their territory.

The Black Sheep Has Favor

Yes, you've got it! Leaders that expand their territory are labeled the black sheep! The black sheep is one that does not follow the social norm which controls their growth. God does not operate in normalcy where man becomes complacent far too many times. We may also view this as favor. Favor isn't fair but it's of God.

Favor is what Joshua received from God. Joshua's leader, Moses, could not enter the Promise Land however he was armed with the authority of God. You have to assess the knowledge of the territory from a high. This is the dwelling place of eagles. Eagles soar high and live in high places where they watch not only their prey, but the entire land. The eagle does not dwell in the area of the common buzzards. The buzzards are only eating the dead that's left for them. The buzzards don't even work for their food, they just wait until it dies and then feeds off the road kill. The eagle feeds off life that God has prepared for their survival. The territory that you observe is full of life. When you subdue it, you feed upon life and advancement. You feed upon the Promised Land of God.

Your inheritance is the Promised Land. You cannot get to the Promised Land if you do not obey the order of God. The fear and running away of your calling is not obedience. You cannot fulfill your purpose if you do not hide in the mountains and wait. Your waiting period in the high places is preparing you for the acquisition of the territory God has promised you. The only way to inherit what God has for us is to follow the rules of God's order. When you follow God's order, there will be agents who will help conceal your mission as God used Rahab to hide the spies. This is also another precedence set here. Do not deny the help God sends you while you're on your way because it doesn't come wrapped in the appearance of what you think it should be. Rahab was the unlikely help that no one would consider to be valuable for Joshua to seize the Promised Land. God continues to show us that there is promise and value in everyone. He uses us all despite our dispositions. He uses us not all the time for our sake but for the sake of greater means.

THE RULE 2:22
PRINCIPLE

(NEW TESTAMENT)

THE RULE 2:22
PRINCIPLE

(CHAPTER SEVENTEEN)

CORRUPTED
CONSUMPTION

CORRUPTED CONSUMPTION

The quickest way to destroy your longevity is to consume the corrupted things of this world. These corrupted things come in the form of ideals, interpretations of spiritual instructions with carnal understandings, thoughts, ways of life, etc. The consumption of your physical as well as your spiritual make up is endanger of being corrupted with every moment not spent in the bosom of God. You can affix yourselves to the ideals of man as a recipe for success but if it's not grounded in the foundation of God, you will lose out. I don't care how successful you are in the material world you will be bankrupt in the spiritual affairs of God.

Touch Not; Taste Not; Handle Not

Colossians *2:22 Which all are to perish with the using :) after the commandments and doctrines of men?*

(Let's back up to verse 20-22.) *20. Wherefore if ye be dead with Christ from the rudiments of the world, why, as though living in the world, are ye subject to ordinances, 21. (Touch not: taste not handle not; 22. Which all are to perish with the using :) after the commandments and doctrines of men?*

You can actually expect to gain nothing living by the rules of the world seeking rewards from God. Buying into the false teachings of the world that resemble the Gospel is a trap that we too often take up a likening vice the foundation of God. You may wonder why you keep seeing the phrase "the foundation of God," well just know that nothing in existence is without the foundation of its creation except that it came through God's creativity. Should you find this true we can understand that God didn't create bad but man took good and used it for other than its purpose and that became the bad.

As we died with Christ and received His victory of the cross over the spiritual powers, we stand free from the evil spiritual powers of this world. Our conversion was death as we died to the world and took up life in Christ. Death did well to separate us from this world as was the Colossians who were separated from the rudiments of the world. There lay a constant battle of believers oppressed by the law of the land rules and regulations that are extremely antiquated as we are under the grace of Christ. Believers are encouraged to stop believing and come into a knowing Christ to make our relationships more intrinsic. Build your faith in Christ that the test of time will prove it worthy.

Scripture tells us touch not; taste not; and handle not these traps of the world as the Gnostics had lain their rules and regulations to set themselves apart from the rest of the world. Christians should be encouraged that we stand liberated through Christ from having to abide by these irrelevant ideals. If we would place our obedience in the keeping of these rules and regulations we would gain the honor of man and lose the honor of God. This is a challenge for many that lack identity in Christ. We follow the principles of success of men based upon their trendsetting actions and mindsets quickly abandoning the path of God. We find more value in being seen and exhorted in worldly matters but shy away from being honored by God as an anointed warrior of Christ.

We don't find any prestige in being obedient to God. We don't find any self-gratification that's needed to boost low self-esteem in the obedience to God. We don't find any outward publically applauded affairs in our obedience to God. But because we don't see it, does this mean that it doesn't exist? No! What has happened is we have become spiritually blinded to all that is good and perfect for us and to us. We are walking around with blinders on. We only see what's in front of us because we've let the world tell us where we can look, when we can look, how we can look, why we must look a certain way, and what to look for.

Abandon the Ordinances of Man

Scripture encourages us that we are free from earthly ordinances and safe in Christ. We feel that if we can see through the bars on our brains we are free. Circumspectly we advance in the kingdom of God by obedience and serving in our purpose for the purpose of being obedient to God. So again, those that have stacked up much material gain generally still find themselves continuously stacking up things trying to fill the empty voids of their spirits. They are perishing and continuing to collect material items believing that it will patch the holes in their spiritual crevices. This is similar to placing a Band-Aid on a crack in a dam. Water is sprouting out of the cracks in the dam and you continue to put Band-Aids over the cracks but the water continues to pour through the cracks expanding the cracks into holes.

If you don't fill the holes with more cement and properly stop the water, your walls will crumble. The dam will perish and your entire existence will be flooded. We can't have bubblegum faith in God. We have to have longevity and longsuffering in our death to this world. If you really want to receive the advancement of Christ you better prepare yourself to be tested time and time again. Dying in Christ has its rewards just as it has its oppositions. The will and the word of men has no place in the Kingdom of God. The childish lessons and elementary spirituality that we boast about is nothing. They do not stand a chance in the world.

Be careful who you let direct your life other than God. The steps of a righteous man are ordered by God, while the steps of a lost man are ordered by other lost men. Learn the doctrine of Christ and avoid the accolades of false teachers that promote a life or religious way of life that is fashioned for God. These appear trustworthy but are in all actuality a means of self-promotion and not a life of humbleness.

We have to mentally destroy the ordinances because this is where the real prison develops. Once the mind accepts the prison ordinances of men it becomes a done deal. The deal is that I will follow you man because God is taking too long to give me access. God is taking too long for me to have the material things. God is taking too long to show me off. God is just taking too long…..He is just taking too long! We have missed the boat! God was building patience in us. God was building our faith. God was building the warrior in us.

God was destroying the ordinances of men by allowing your obedience to conquer the strongholds that plague your life. God was building a relationship with you that would stand the test of time and all trials and tribulations. The answer lies within you, whether you will perish from corrupted consumptions or live in Christ.

THE RULE 2:22
PRINCIPLE

(CHAPTER EIGHTEEN)

CLEAN YOUR TEMPLE

CLEAN YOUR TEMPLE

In this day and age we quickly arrive at the thought of cleaning your temple only to mean eat healthy and do some type of dieting or fasting. Here, Rule 2:22 will go just a level or so in depth beyond what we recognize on the surface. Cleaning your temple means to clean up everything within sight and hearing of your environment and presence of wherever you find yourself. Living in righteousness does not mean that we are righteous however it points to the fact that where we tread in this world is filled with unrighteousness and therefore we must be the servant custodian continuously cleansing the temple of God (the world) no matter where we find ourselves.

How then can we be clean living in filthy environments of operations but carry a clean mind, body, and spirit? Picture the presence of an all-white robe hanging in the middle of a whirlwind of dust flying about. Surely the presence of the all-white robe continues to illuminate from amongst the whirlwind of dust, however, there are unseen particles that have attached themselves to the surface of the robe. Eventually if the robe is not removed from the dust storm, it will become saturated with so much dust that the pores of the fabric will begin to soak up the particles of dust and the surface of the robe will commit itself to the tainting of the dust.

Your temple is much like that of the robe. As you press towards the mark of the high calling of God, you will venture into unclean territories that you must go in order to serve God. However, you or we have to continue to cleanse our temples. We must be mindful that although we feel that we have not been infected, we still carry microscopic thoughts that have entered our ear-gates and eye-gates which can damage our mainframe (the brain). One of the greatest mistakes we can make is not acknowledging the fact that we are still flesh and bone subject to sin. You don't have to participate in the sin to be touched you can just be in the presence and feel the spirit of uncleanness. Soon, the filth of sin will penetrate the crevices of your armor if you never conduct preventive maintenance. You have to seal the cracks in your armor to clean your temple.

The Physical Cleansing

John 2:22 When therefore he was risen from the dead, his disciples remembered that he had said this unto them; and they believed the scripture, and the word which Jesus had said. When Jesus ordered the destruction of the temple many could only focus on their own biases in wanting to acknowledge the 46 years the temple has been standing. The people couldn't understand how the temple could be rebuilt in just three short days because the filth of sin had limited their minds to the surface level understanding of Jesus' message. Christ was speaking to the terms of destruction to His body and His resurrection from the dead. The dust particles of sin had far penetrated their minds and infected their righteous understanding of The Great One. The physical temple was merely the symbolism of His body and the purpose of the Jewish Temple would be destroyed with the destroying of Jesus' body.

A cleaning will come whether you lead the cleaning crew or not. If you don't clean your temples regularly, what comes into the temple will clean you from its existence. Either you establish the presence of your cleansing the temple or the temple of filth shall establish a monument of where you used to stand. The disciples began to realize that this is what Jesus had spoken of long before this time. They saw that His words were coming to pass. Their travels had led them through dust storms that had even slightly tainted their wisdom in Jesus. Jesus was the servant constantly cleansing their temples or environment surrounding them. When you continuously walk in the presence of the Lord you are cleansing your temple.

The Spiritual Cleansing

Don't get trapped into the physical existence of your nature that you disregard the spirituality of your presence. What you see and feel on the outer shell is the direct result of what lies on the inside of the shell. If you experience pain on the outside of the shell it is because your internal shell has communicated that aspect to inform you that you should feel pain. Your outside should not control your inside however your inside should control your outside. Keep in mind the scriptures tell us that the spirit is willing but the flesh is weak. So as tough as the skin is it can also become metaphorically a weak covering of the inside.

What's on the inside of your temple? Are you physically impaired on the outside because you're spiritually impaired on the inside? As Jesus' death was a sign of transformation and the approval that came through His resurrection, we must understand that our temples need to be spiritually cleansed. We reside in the Word of God, not just treading the scriptures with redundancy, and thinking we will not be infected by the brutal sin attacks that surround us. Keep the faith. Keeping the faith is more than just saying "I believe." "I believe" is short of saying you haven't witnessed a change however you are keeping the hope that you might witness change at some point. Keeping the faith is "knowing." This means your faith has been tried and withstood the vicissitudes of life.

The Jews could not see pass taking Christ in a literal sense and therefore omitted any type of spiritual reflection or acknowledgement of Christ's statement. More so, the disciples witnessed spiritual cleansing in the events of the resurrection of Christ. The disciples all died to their physical understanding and were reborn in their spiritual awareness. Their physical temples had to be cleansed from the inner spirit in order to receive an outer impact of being cleaned. They believed Jesus as long as Jesus was amongst them because the world had taught them to believe in what they could see. This was symbolically the dust over their eyes and minds that needed to be cleaned. Jesus' resurrection brought about a cleansing of their spirits as their eyes were now open to greater things.

Carnal ramifications are most likely to hinder any form of spiritual advancement in believers. Spiritual advancements are restricted by unclean temples. What you allow in your spirit not of God steals, kills, and destroys the greatest potential of your spirit. Yes the spirit is willing but it must maintain the true pulchritude of Christ in order to reflect the light of Christ. So as we understand that Christ's words "make not my father's house a house of merchandise," we can metaphorically analyze the idea of how we have made our temples places of merchandise as we have sold the spirit of God out to the physicality of the world.

The forty six years of the Jewish Temple existence is characterized as the essence of man's age and nature. The forty six years represent to us that regardless of the age of a person, Christ can still destroy and rebuild man in any state of being. It doesn't matter how long you have been outside the realm of Christ because you can be restored or resurrected with perfection through Christ in the very moment you confess your sins unto Christ and accept Him as your Lord and Savior. You don't have to worry about how long you've been on a strange path needing to dedicate or rededicate yourself, just know that God is the Creator of time. He owns and operates time according to His will and not that of our own.

Never let your eyes deceive your heart. Your heart should control what you allow your eyes to see. A lot of times what we think we see is as truth, our heart tells us that it's not true but we rely solely on the physical presence of the object and not the spiritual superiority of God's omniscience. He is all knowing! He that is all-knowing is the spiritual provider for us all. The challenge we face is cleaning up every temple or place we come into with the Word of God. Let us together cleanse the temple of God and affirm to a daily cleaning of our temples.

THE RULE 2:22
PRINCIPLE

(CHAPTER NINETEEN)

PURIFY YOUR PURPOSE

PURIFY YOUR PURPOSE

Your purpose is not only unique for you but others stand in wait for you to purify your purpose as to free them from their uncleanness. The unclean nature of this world has been covered by sin and misdirection. Misdirection comes at the hands of unclean spirits that cause us to veer from the purpose God has created us to fulfill. Let us understand that fulfilling your purpose is the free will living God has allowed us to live as He has given us the instructional manual called The Holy Bible. It is God that presents you blameless and faultless before the world. We don't and further can't present ourselves in this manner. The revealing of your purposeful overcoming the uncleanness is relevant to all that know of your inception.

Many of us live in unclean environments that seek to keep us attached to ungodly written laws that hinder the fulfillment of our purpose. Destiny is nothing if we fail to realize the purpose of reaching our destinies. Your destiny is encompassed in the pre-thought of your destination. Your purpose is never tainted it is your destiny that suffers the attacks of unclean pathways filled with filth. You stand to sanctify the presence of those from which you come, if you can only purify your purpose under the calling of God.

Moment of Purification

Luke 2:22 And when the days of her purification according to the law of Moses were accomplished, they brought him to Jerusalem, to present him to the Lord: The moment of purification was made known when an angel appeared making the announcement of the Savior's birth to the lowly shepherds. The Savior was the promised one of the Old Testament. The Savior was to be known as the Deliverer, the Anointed One (Messiah), and even the Lord Himself.

The purification of your purpose is likened unto the birth of the Savior. The Savior would represent the coming of a clean spirit to wipe away or end the unclean situations of the people. According to the Old Testament, Mary's uncleanness lasted forty days after the birth of Jesus. The circumcision of a male child would take away some of the uncleanness and a female birth would cause the uncleanness to last for eighty days. Your moment of purification is in the masculine male birth that will defeat the uncleanness of your environment.

The moment you comprehend your purpose it is the moment you suffer not the deterrence. The moment you purify your purpose you activate the God spirit in you and no one can hinder your strides, no one can break your momentum, no one can steal your motivation, no one can darken your path, and no one can convince you that you will not fulfill your purpose. It is in that precise moment the world around you feels the trembling of the ground as you become the earthquake of God's promise over your life. This is the moment the symbolic lava of the Holy Spirit begins to bubble within you and seeks to pour out unto all that are in proximity of your eruption. The effects of your eruption though not seen are forever sketched in the cannons of history. Your purpose is felt throughout and acknowledged as God's fulfillment of His promise. This moment of purification is the cleansing of unclean demeanors and effortless behaviors of maturity. This process is warranted and sanctioned by God.

The Presentation of Purpose

If we're not careful in our lack of understanding our purpose we will be confused by the process by which our purpose is fulfilled. Patience is a virtue. Your purpose is not all the time comprehended at the pace as many others that have received their calling and understand their purpose in life. This does not mean that God favored them more than you. This simply means that your purpose is uniquely designed for you and no one else. The presentation of your purpose must and will go through the complimentary stages of testing.

After an eight year old Jesus had been circumcised, it was approximately five weeks later that Mary and Joseph traveled five miles to the temple of Jerusalem to offer the sacrifice required by Moses in Leviticus 12. The process by which the fulfillment of Jesus' purpose would capture the purpose of others in the wake of the greatest promise fulfilled ever. In the process of Jesus' presentation, Mary and Joseph's purpose was being presented also. They would be the Godly elected persons created to bring forth and provide the world with our beloved Savior. We can overlook the purposes of others being fulfilled by simply looking at our own purposes. Thankfully Jesus was not of this character.

If you really want to fulfill your purpose in life, you must first understand that others are not only affected by your purpose but they are also fulfilling their purpose. The balance of life will not have one without the other. The presentation of your purpose gives hope to others. The presentation of you purifying your purpose sheds the myths that plague the fulfillment of so many peoples' purposes. Amongst the presentation of purpose stands God Himself. Prior to Christ's birth, Simeon was informed by the Holy Spirit that he would behold the longed promised Messiah before he died. Simeon spoke of Jesus as the light of the gentiles and the glory of Israel. These actions and statements were merely overlooked promises fulfilled by God that would prove true as Jesus had come to fulfill His purpose.

We must understand that along the path of purpose-filling, we will encounter purpose filled people that also will be presented unto the world by God. It is our duty to fulfill our purpose that others may fulfill their purpose. We are all constructively and creatively affixed in one another's lives to present matters and situations that not only test our purpose-filled lives, but shine light on the purification process that purpose is born from. What will you not fulfill when you acknowledge your purpose? You will shatter the dimensions of uncleanness and promote a purification process that will always promote promise fulfillment.

"No one should ever stop you from living for God. Living for God is exercising every bit of ability He has granted you in Jesus name."

THE RULE 2:22 PRINCIPLE

(CHAPTER TWENTY)

EMBRACE YOUR DREAMS

EMBRACE YOUR DREAMS

Wisdom comes to us through various means. God communicates to all of us through animals, experiences, people, places, things, etc. The world of believers would even have those that debate whether God speaks to those that are not saved. If we would ponder just one short moment, we would consider that God most definitely communicates to all of us because there are many times in all of our lives that something brings about a thought to let us know that we aren't under the arc of safety. However we intend to account for these experiences, it happens. The wisest of us would heed and not hesitate to follow the safety of what God exposes to us. For those of us that choose the alternate path, we find that protection is the least concern of ours when we seek to live for the world and not for the safety of our beings.

Warning in a Dream

Matthew 2:22 But when he heard that Archelaus did reign in Judea in the room of his father Herod, he was afraid to go thither: notwithstanding, being warned of God in a dream, he turned aside into the parts of Galilee:

Joseph has now received God's guidance through a dream telling him to avoid venturing to Judea. Archelaus, Herod's son is now the successor of the kingship and is even more brutal than his father. What should be taken from this is the fact that this is a second dream of warning by God given to Joseph to protect the life of Jesus. As Jesus was born in Bethlehem of Judea the wise men were alerted and guided by a star in the east. Jesus is revealed to be the King of the Jews or a governor that shall rule the people of Israel prophesized by the prophet. When Herod learns of this, his envy and jealousy leads him to devise a plot to destroy Jesus. Herod tells the wise men to locate Jesus as he wishes to appear before Jesus to honor him which is merely a plot to kill him.

Ask yourself, how many dreams revealed a change of circumstances that I did not heed to that caused me harm. Ask yourself, how many dreams have been revealed to me that I have ignored the red flags in my life that caused me to hinder my progress. Ask yourself, how many dreams have God given me that awaken me to the conscience of life but I found no change of heart. The thought that you are having right now is a conscience of God that every man has that he either draws to or runs from as God speaks to him. Often times there are fears that cause us not to heed to the presence of God based upon our lack of understanding the availability of God. God is not a movie that ends.

God is not an author who has reached a mind-block that cannot give you vision to purposely fulfill your destiny.

You're probably losing focus appealing to that inner you that ask the question, who can interpret dreams. I want to warn you that your ability to reason what your dreams mean is still God giving you a conscience. You are conscious! Where we are is not our end nor is it God's plan to keep us where we come to life. God propels us into safety through dreams. How we react to our dreams can be the greatest accomplishment of our lives. Let your dreams give you life and not death. Joseph understood his dreams not to be just weary thoughts but acts of God's grace to render Jesus protection. Joseph could have second guessed his dreams but I wish to bring you to another level of thought. If God is allowing you to dream, then you must understand that God is communicating with you even in your lack of understanding. Your survival to fulfill your purpose will be your reaction to your

dreams.

The Plight to Kill Your Dreams

We must all go to God for the wisdom to interpret

our dreams. Our dreams have been categorized by the

world as dimensional glimpses sometimes prompted by

what we eat, when we eat, or thinking over obsessively

about a thing. However we decided to acknowledge our

dreams, God is the keeper of our dreams. God is the

conscious part of our dreams that allows us the ability

to seek a greater understanding of who we are, what our

purpose is, and what we wonder about His purpose in

allowing us to dream. If we could eliminate our

personal wants while dreaming we could see a greater

purpose behind our dreams.

The lack of knowledge we bear of our dreams

symbolizes Herod. Herod seeks to keep us from the

purpose God has over our lives. In our dreaming, we access greater purpose. There are periods of time in our lives where we go without dreaming. Does this mean that God is not communicating with us, No! This apparent break in our life of dreaming is simply another process in God's communication with us. We need meditation time for our dreams to manifest and grow towards God's intended purpose. Joseph's guiding his family around to safe havens enabled Jesus to grow and fulfill God's purpose over his life.

There are a multitude of Herods in this world. They hear of your dreams and they seek to plan your destruction. They know that your dreams will also spell out protection for others. Jesus's birth also meant that others would be involved to bring about a course of action necessary for humanity. If Herod can keep you from dreaming, then he can kill your purpose. If Herod can keep you from dreaming, he can cripple a nation. If

Herod can keep you from dreaming, he can write you off as a failure. If Herod can keep you from dreaming, he can ensure that you will not accept what God has for you. And if Herod can keep you from dreaming, he knows that you will never heed to the instruction that will keep you safe and under God's wings of protection.

THE RULE 2:22 PRINCIPLE

(CHAPTER TWENTY ONE)

LET THE NEW WINE OF YOUR MIND FLOW

LET THE NEW WINE OF YOUR MIND FLOW

Some of the most brilliant minds have gone on to make significant strides in the world such as Sir Isaac Newton, Albert Einstein, Martin Luther King, Jr., and yes, even President Barak Obama. Each in their own right has stretched the normalcy ushering in the new or expansion, which the world only knew to have a conditioned limitation. The adherence of law contains your growth and tells you when and if you can grow. Your mind is the only thing that can set you free from the old sanctions that keep you unproductively declining each day of your life.

Your old friends, your old stomping grounds, your old jobs, your old schools, your old teachers, and your old loves collectively have positioned you for growth however they are also the laws that you have grounded yourself by to give you what you believe are the foundations of expansion. As we meticulously venture through life in high hopes of achieving ambitions, we find that our new life thinking disrupts the old sanctions that created our outlook on life. We find that new principles stretch the very structure or blueprint we were raised on. We find ourselves realizing the ability to not settle and to proactively seek new opportunities vice those that come our way without any effort whatsoever. We reluctantly press the limits of those controllable factors we were taught to embrace. However as we reluctantly oppose those thoughts, we know that in the end, it creates greater for the totality of humankind.

Bursting Old Wineskins

Mark 2:22 "And no one puts new wine into old wineskins; or else the new wine bursts the wineskins, the wine is spilled, and the wineskins are ruined. But new wine must be put into new wineskins." Essentially

Mark breaks down this principle with the relativity of fasting here. New cloth and new wine are presented for a relevant understanding of how we can stretch the environments that we are technically a product of. The new cloth which hasn't been preshrunk will tear away from old cloth that has reached its limitation. New wine is not settled and therefore expands as it ages. The commercials for wine these days promote wine getting better with time. Again, when we understand that the old wineskins have reached their limits, we also see that aging will cause expansion and therefore old wineskins will eventually burst from having reached its limits.

This principle of Rule 2:22 urge us to constantly strengthen or toughen our old skin as we will be pushed to limits beyond that of our traditional upbringings. We cannot allow medial unproductive attacks on our character to distract us from our goals. We cannot embrace unproductive gatherings of those minds that continuously seek to draw us into their environments of diseased devices that seek to kill our momentum in creating greater for the sake of all humanity. Jesus stretched the Old Testament law of murder as it had reached its physical limitations, by presenting New Testament outlook that man commits murder if he is found hating. We wouldn't dare compare mental murdering to physical murdering in today's time but if we were to stop and think, we would find that the seed was first planted in the mind by some form of decisive or intrusive hate for something that caused the murder to be carried out. The pure of heart will only produce purity. Those that are infected and infested with seeds of hate, also seek to ravish those pure at hearts seeking to spread love, joy, and peace

Don't Be Restricted in Your Work

When we serve God there are no restrictions to our working hours. Many of people would like to tell us that it doesn't take all that. When people say it doesn't take all that, we should ask ourselves what are they really asking or better yet, what are they really saying to us. In other words, they are saying there are limits to the amount of service to God that we should conduct. I wish to tell us that as long as we do the norm we are good in our works. Likewise, those that don't share the same passion for our destinies will begin to set limits for our work. Students that generally find themselves in graduate schools find that friends and family become very significant distractions to their studies because they feel like they are just working extremely hard and need a break. Realistically, we know that even the time that we're not around them we still slack from the actual studying we should be putting forth. When they

324

say take a break, what they are really saying is come party with us or come hangout with us and you'll be alright. It's sad to say that even Christians will distract us with the same kind of statements.

The Pharisees questioned the principle of not working on the Sabbath as Jesus and disciples walked through the corn fields and the disciples plucked ears of corn. Instead of understanding what it took or what it required of them, the Pharisees only saw the ears of corn being plucked so that they could hold Jesus and the disciples to the law of not working on the Sabbath. You can easily become distracted by these chants of deceit simply because of traditional means that masses of people follow. However, those that desire more from God and life realize that you can't settle for average if you expect to accomplish much more in life. Those that are highly successful do sacrifice much time but they also get to reap the rewards of their sacrifices. Those that are faithfully employed to service are rewarded with the blessings of increase.

When we let others put restrictions on what we are working towards then we settle for what they want in their lives and not that of our own. I remember I used to have family members tell me all the time that I needed to relax and not work so hard but they didn't realize that I had goals that I wished to accomplish. By them not being able to align themselves with the work ethic it took to acquire those things we hoped for, it crippled our family as a whole. We just continued to struggle more and more. I would like to say that just because you work hard doesn't always mean that you'll be successful because you can work hard in unprogressive means that produce no fruit. Visions and missions have to be aligned in order to accomplish projects. The principle of Rule 2:22 is old skins will be stretched tremendously by the exercising of mindful thoughts of new wine. The old skins have become limited because of their environments. Their wills have been seized and squeezed dry of their entrepreneurial and proactive leadership. They fall into dimensions of inactive behaviors spawning only limited affairs. You are encouraged to "let the new wine of your mind flow." If President Obama believed what the world of normalcy spoke to him, then he never would have become the 44th President of the United States of America. The cycle of tradition must be broken in order for us to reach limitless fields of progression providing better for people as a whole.

We are the new wine! We are not limited as our old skins have become robbed of their dreams and visions. We are the new wine that expands with time as we continue to trust God for exceedingly and abundantly giving us the increase of tomorrow. We trust in Him and Him alone to pour us as new wine into an old world needing change. We see this in Jesus Christ as he was poured into an old world to bring forth new vision. Today we still reap the rewards of Him getting better with time and expanding spiritually through the world.

THE RULE 2:22 PRINCIPLE

(CHAPTER TWENTY TWO)

REFLECT WHAT YOU PREACH AND TEACH

REFLECT WHAT YOU PREACH AND TEACH

This principle is one that many of us were indirectly taught but directly forced to take on since youth. Parents don't realize the impact they have on their children when they argue, "do as I say and not as I do." If they meant it from the positive prospective of don't do the wrong that I do and do the good that I don't do it would be profound. However, we learn earlier on that parents or simply adults feel they can live as they wish to live regardless of it being right or wrong, but when their children become wise to their sins and speak on it, the conviction drives them to stand on the adult platform to elude their guilt.

Preaching the Law but Not Living by the Law

Dating back to the earlier Jews of the law they took on the same attitudes and characters that plague society today. Paul was very instrumental in pointing out that

330

the Jews would teach others to abide by the laws but fail to abide by the very laws they sought to enforce. The Jews condemned the Gentiles which they regarded as heathens instructing them to be law abiding citizens while they the Jews continuously broke the laws.

Romans 2:22 Thou that sayest a man should not commit adultery, dost thou commit adultery? Thou that abhorrest idols, dost thou commit sacrilege?

The question went out to the Jews why were they so willing to preach morality when their lives did not support the message they preached. The Jews were found to be stealing from each other, committing adultery, and they were profaning the house of God through commercializing behaviors. Knowing the laws and enforcing them then not living by them placed the Jews in the position to be known as hypocrites.

Character Reflection

In order to have a character that is well respected with integrity you have to practice what you preach and teach even when it convicts you. If we could learn to preach on or from a format that exposes that we are not infallible, we could reach more people with the Gospel of Christ. The reason being is that many of convicted, struggling unsaved souls as well as saved souls battle with themselves not measuring up to the messages they hear week after week in bible studies and church services. They see the leadership of the church as being the head that never veers from the path of righteousness while the rest of the congregation suffers the weakness of sin.

Disconnecting people from who they are and who we are supposed to be working towards the same goal or vision can be crippling all at the same time. People don't have a problem really admitting that they are wrong, but what they do have a problem in doing is admitting their guilt why the other party acts as if they have been "holy art thou" preachers. When I say preacher I'm not just speaking of the one that graces the pulpit but I speak to the ones that are in places of leadership, management, supervision or even instructs others.

If you don't want to be scrutinized then leadership is not the place for you. What you do and speak will come under scrutiny often. Your credibility lies within being able to admit when you're wrong as much as gloating when you're right. Sadly, many of our lives have not been shaped by those that readily stand to promote their wrongdoings as much as those that played major parts in our lives that bolstered self-centered behaviors and having entitlement issues. So when we say that the youth are just out of control what we really should say is that we propelled them initially to be out of control.

Egoism

Perhaps if we would make greater attempts at destroying our egos, we could be more of a vessel that seeks to live an exemplary life of Christ. Our egos keep us from wanting to demean our perceived character. Actually our egos are what cause us to break the laws from the start. Just think! Why is it that we know the law but believe we are bigger than the law or the rules and regulations given to guide us in order? We also feel that when people are not aware of us breaking laws then we haven't broken laws.

This is an example of our egoism. One of the loosely descriptive definitions of egoism is it treats self-interest as a foundation of morality for the particular person. There are a large portion of the human population that from one means or another live by this code of egoism because they feel it gives them protection from being seen as weak. Society makes us believe that admitting guilt for wrong is a sign of weakness in our character, position, and statue. Egoism destroys rationale. Egoism locks the door to objective reasoning. Egoism promotes subjective reasoning all at the hands of having the ball in one's court for so-called fair play.

What are we really seeking to accomplish with the arrogant egos that we display? I often look at the people that are quick to establish that others have egos and wonder do they see themselves as having egos. Have they really stopped and analyzed themselves to see that their egotistical dispositions breed a character defect of entitlement as well. They are preaching destroy the egoism however they're not abiding by the practice of what they are preaching. This becomes tough when we become so readily equipped to just tell people off. Where's the humbleness of character that doesn't fall short as we are seeking to issue constructive criticism? Or are we really just getting our egotistical rocks off at the expensive of someone else's egotistical defaults. Either way, practicing this principle causes us to scrutinize our behaviors much more before acting or speaking out to correct people.

Adapting to the Principle

If we were to adapt to this principle, there would be increasingly less divorces, less family quarrels, less work order disruption, less police brutality, less community violence, and less world violence. Sure this all sounds far-fetched but if we would all start with ourselves, we could see the effects of this principle bring a positive change to our personal as well as collective situations. What is my attitude becomes more of what we should ask ourselves. Do we wish to be of those that only talk a good game and walk as a lame or do we see ourselves in the light of Christ preaching and teaching others through our actions, reflecting a more god-centered presence? This question has to be answered by every reader and then acted upon if the correcting which needs to be done is to be effective.

On any given day you can find law enforcement officers speeding through busy streets appearing to be answering a call, some with flashing lights and some without, but regardless of the perception only they know whether they are on official duty with the right to speed. What many don't realize is that even officers are governed by the same law that they issue citations for. They are to proceed with due caution exercising safety for themselves and the public. The flashing lights should be on each time a call is being answered and speeds are increased. The flashing lights are to warn the public that they need access to the streets and they are seeking to excel with obstruction to attend to their duties.

Unfortunately, the officer that writes the most citations for speeding are generally just as guilty of speeding violations on and off duty. Now here's where the integrity part of the matter comes into play. How many believing officers are willing to admit that they are breaking the law consistently and continuously without being reprimanded for their action? It all goes back to are we reflecting what we preach and teach. After stopping a law violator and issuing them a citation for speeding, an officer may find himself consciously and unconsciously speeding in excess heading to go set up for the next possible violator. I saved this for now because I was guilty for this same matter when I used to be a law enforcement officer. It's just amazing how many laws you break that you write citations for.

You will find this behavior in every profession in the world. However we choose to justify our actions, we are all opposing the very principle that we say we uphold. We have critically fallen into the "do as I say but not as I do" category. Should we all one day decide to conduct ourselves as we truly know God is continuously watching us, then and only then will we reflect the true meaning of reflect what you preach and teach.

Before our actions are to be set forth we should view this for what the real value is. The real value in this is credited to honoring God. Should we boast the law in God and honor it, we preach and teach to the world unconditionally the righteousness of God and better living. We create a world mirror by which every person would see himself or herself as the model of a reflection or law and obedience.

THE RULE 2:22 PRINCIPLE

(CHAPTER TWENTY THREE)

RECIPROCAL AFFECTION

RECIPROCAL AFFECTION

Loyalty is not the efforts of the subordinate to support the master in the lack of his duties or wrongdoings. Loyalty is not the efforts of the master to underhandedly suppress the subordinate because God has gifted him. Loyalty is reciprocated and not used by the senior to maintain his position because he wishes not to lose his position, for the fear that his days are numbered, or that he may even lose the favor of the people. Loyalty is the value of a mutual companionship where the senior as well as the junior reciprocate the worthiness of both parties to serve God in such a way that they give each other the best support that one could ever receive or give.

In order to examine this proven worth, both parties have to put aside their personal ideas or ambitions and focus on the goal of God. The goal of God should be the focal point of the companionship. If one or both parties ever begin to think they are losing something in the companionship then they will lack in serving God and fail each other. We see enough of this in church leadership today. Ongoing struggles of elder pastors living out their leadership days stand in fear of young strong ministers only seeking to serve the Lord. Young ministers are forced to live under the authoritative leadership claiming they don't know anything and believe they are rushing and not prepared.

Likewise, young ministers see their elder leadership as out of touch and irrelevant to the budding congregation they desire to see. Often young ministers are frustrated by the process of these ungodly tactics they are forced to live through in just wishing to serve. Elder pastors view this or at least claim that young ministers have no loyalty to them. Young ministers tend to fall away from leadership that doesn't let them express the gifts God has blessed them with. All the same, both sides need a balance in understanding what God has set in place for the companionship that bears loyalty.

Proof of Loyalty

Philippians 2:22 But ye know the proof of him, that, as a son with the father, he hath served with me in the gospel. The incredible leadership that Paul has provided for Timothy set the foundation for Timothy to reciprocate a loyalty and allegiance unto Paul that was unmatched by many. Timothy's loyalty to not just Paul but to God has been tried, tested and proven to be worthy of honor. Paul has approved of Timothy's commitment to a godly life.

Make no mistake in the exegesis of this text that Paul afforded Timothy opportunities, as well as encouraged and supported all his efforts during the course of their relationship. The personal relationship shared between Paul and Timothy was one of reciprocated affection for each other. The mutual respect for the positioning was grandiose because these two warriors for Christ did not lose focus in lieu of trying to accomplish some self-serving accolade.

We find throughout other scriptures of the gospel that Paul encouraged Timothy to go forth and preach the gospel in and out of season even when Timothy doubted his own ability or doubted what other elders of the church would think of him due to his age and time in the gospel.

Reciprocating Your Loyalty

Unfortunately reciprocated loyalty amongst men is viewed as them covering each other whether it be by rightful or wrongful means. Men have destroyed this valuable loyalty because they think more of themselves and not more of the Kingdom building that should be priority. *2 Timothy 3:2-4 reads, "For men shall be lovers of their own selves, covetous, boasters, proud, blasphemers, disobedient to parents unthankful, unholy, without natural affection, trucebreakers, false accusers, incontinent, fierce, despisers of those that are good, traitors, heady, high-minded, lovers of pleasure rather than lovers of God;*

Loyalty must start within self. If you cheat yourself out of anything in life then you are always subject to cheat others. Sin is the key element that man faces which will make him vulnerable to a lack of loyalty that he needs for himself and others. Men lack tremendous amounts of loyalty to God but demand much more loyalty for themselves from other men. Men engage in treaty making mostly to prosper and not to serve the welfare of all people. To make things even clearer, women should be warned that this includes them also.

If one is to begin to display loyalty then he or she must develop some personal disciplines about themselves. They must first commit to serving God in such a way that their integrity will not be compromised by man when placed in awkward positions. This means that a job, money, promises, or any other means will not manipulate their stance of being loyal. We have to develop the faith in God that will not let us fear what man does not own.

People will make you feel like leaving them is the worst thing in the world and God will not bless you. I speak from personal experiences that had I not left certain situations I would have missed what God had for me. I now respect any and everything I thought was bad and good that happened to me. It took a balance of pain and pleasure to make Aqeel Ash-Shakoor who he has become today. I'm even able to forgive others much faster and quicker in heart than I was previously. The

346

hurt held me back because of the way I viewed it, while at the same time learning to live with it and not in it, as it propelled me forward. It helped me mature in being more loyal to God. Although I have a much further way to go, I'm joyful that I'm learning it.

The loyalty that is needed for a reciprocated affection amongst people is the bread and butter between understanding "where two or three are gathered in the name of Christ" will bring into fruition more miracles, signs, and wonders of Jesus. Advancement is hindered when we lack the loyalty of reciprocation. We should never look for loyalty in people that we have not ourselves invested thoroughly in honoring God. Marriages, business relationships, friends, family members, and church members stand to benefit tremendously; mentally, physically, and spiritually should they practice and improve in the reciprocal affection for one another.

THE RULE 2:22 PRINCIPLE

(CHAPTER TWENTY FOUR)

SPEAK OUT CONCERNING MIRACLES, WONDERS, AND SIGNS

SPEAK OUT CONCERNING MIRACLES, WONDERS, AND SIGNS

Probably one of the most shameful acts we do as believers is to not go forth and let the miracles of God be known to others. We fail to let our God presence reflect the Word that we say we live by. You even find yourself debating on the thought, "Why am I so afraid to let the God in me shine amongst some people?" Sure it's not something we do around everyone however we don't always go forth with boldness to live a life that reflects the security of our Savior, Jesus Christ. In fact, most self-improvement books or motivational speakers speak from biblical principles but in order to crack the doors of some secular arenas that do and say everything except God or Jesus.

The message is well packaged but the exclamation point of Jesus is missing and therefore the best self-improvement message becomes hype and not hope.

You must learn that you have to stand and stand firm in your walk and not be deterred because you must be crucified in order to fulfill your purpose. It's not until you have risen from the persecution do the masses receive the message in totality or fulfillment of all that proceeded your presence.

Acts 2:22 Ye men of Israel, hear these words; Jesus of Nazareth, a man approved by God among you by miracles and wonders and signs, which God did by him in the midst of you, as ye yourselves also know: It is here that Peter now clings to the death, burial, and resurrection as the meat and potatoes of his message. Peter asserts that the anointed and praise worthy Christ who has worked all signs and wonders through God has been crucified and slain. The persecution of Christ came at the hands and mouths of mobs.

Character Assassination

It is of most importance to tell you that even heavy persecution or assignation of your character is part of the foreknowledge of God to propel you into the destiny that has been prepared for you. Most of us will continue to fight against the plans of God because we seek to take the path of less resistance as spoken of previously. We have to stop thinking of ourselves and serve the people as Christ did. We have to stop being scared to lose a job or position in all efforts to serve the people.

Sometimes in serving the people we have to take a secular loss while simultaneously receiving spiritual prosperity. Jesus suffered death but not murder. God's principle was that Jesus would come and suffer death for us. This was not conditional terms but unconditional favor. Yes every person born unto this world was delighted in favor at least once in their life because

Christ died for all of our sins. Regardless whether or not we all accept Christ as our Lord and Savior, His purpose has been fulfilled.

If you could get your mind off not wanting to die for certain people or stand for certain people, you would become a great server. You would become a modern day-likening to Jesus. If you and every believer could capture the true essence of the principle lain here, we would all benefit from this godly ordained affair. We always try to change the direction of the flow in which God has propelled us to move. We wish to soar like the wind but not go with the flow of the wind.

Your death through the crucifixion of your character is paramount to others' lives. You are merely a servant of the most-high God that is sacrificed to advance the people and not yourself. This is why we must speak out to the ever present miracles, wonders, and signs of God, so that others receive hope in all the turmoil they face.

We cannot walk around in the selfish affairs of this life that we are acting as misers and storing up gifts that belong to the people of the world. The unsaved are starving for God's presence and we are hording the spiritual food that the hungry need.

Come Out From Hiding

Stop hiding your bibles! Stop withholding your testimonies! Stop sneaking to pray to God! Stop breaking your fast to wine and dine with people that have no respect for your God! We must become a people that don't pick and choose when to serve God because they are in certain places or around certain people. The miracles, wonders, and signs of God must be witnessed and seen time and time again, because we live in a society that tries to give credit to luck, rabbit feet, chicken legs, and all sorts of crazy things that bear no power. Anything you receive in this life is by the permission of God. Even that which you receive that is deemed bad is by the means that God allowed you to make a choice to choose between Him and evil. Yes, God could have stopped you but He also gave you knowledge to choose to see if you would be obedient through His repetitious corrections and forgiveness. God does not cause you to go through but He allows you to come out if you should seek His presence through seeking the Kingdom before all things.

Consider the thought that the next person you encounter has an unshared testimony that you need; a divorce, a deceased loved one, a job lose, a terminal illness, or just some sort of setback that would benefit you to instill hope. The unshared miracles, wonders, and signs would serve you in no way if they continue to keep them stored up. Someone is waiting to hear how God cancelled out the cancer that was attacking your body. Someone is waiting to hear how God restored you to even greater after a divorce. Someone is waiting to hear how you are now comforted by the Holy Spirit after the loss of your loved one because you finally received Jesus as the Comforter. Even your enemies can be moved to seek the Lord by the sharing and witnessing of miracles, wonders, and signs of God.

Be a World Changer

If you want to be a world changer all you have to do is exercise the power of your testimony through the authority of God to "go ye therefore into the world and preach the Gospel of Christ." God has given you the authority and the ability to shake off the fear of yourself and others to walk and be the model for His miracles, wonders, and signs. Most that know us might not know every detail of our struggles however they will bear witness to when you receive a come-up. They may not recognize you as you are amongst the normalcy of being on the bottom but they have their own type of shout when they see you on the come up. Some of their shouts are shouts of condemnation at the hands of envy and jealousy but that's just a cry out to witness where God has brought you from.

Their spirit is bearing witness to the favor of God but their flesh is warring with the spirit to glorify God for your breakthrough. That's why you have to smile in the face of your enemies when they attack you, because they are praising you but don't know how to confess that God is an awesome God and He reigns. They keep attacking you because they just can't believe the miracle work of how you may go down but you never stay down at their best attacks, plans, and plots. Our lives should be living testimonies of God's miracles, wonders, and signs.

You don't have to be as famous as Jesus to be used to represent the miracles, wonders, and signs of God's promises. You don't have to be in church leadership. You don't have to be someone that has been in church for forty to fifty years. You can be just as fresh as a new born baby to the world to be an example of miracles, wonders, and signs. You don't have to have the testimony of any other person. The miracles, wonders, and signs of God are not old fashion and neither are they extinct. God's miracles, wonders, and signs are seen well manifested in today's time when you see ex-drug-dealers now profound pastors of prosperous ministries. People that have gone through several heart operations are still defying every doctor's report of limited life.

THE RULE 2:22 PRINCIPLE

(CHAPTER TWENTY FIVE)

MAINTAIN A DWELLING PLACE FOR GOD

MAINTAIN A DWELLING PLACE FOR GOD

I'll be the first to admit that I thought maintaining a dwelling place for God was just simply me saying "I have Him in my heart!" That's also when I began to realize that many other people thought and still think the way I used to think. Very much so, we all believe that our dwelling place for God is the physical church or edifice we attend each week for bible study and weekend services. I also want to tell you that it's not limited to the secret closet that you actually were mistaken for a regular hat and coat closet in your home.

Maintaining a dwelling place for God is a daily duty that gets no holiday, sick or vacation time off. There are no inclement weather call-in or call-out days. There is no separation of pleasure, work or religion. God is not paying rent to dwell within us. We're very unconscious how we treat our Savior like He is a tenant in our rental property when it is vice versa. God has provided us the means of a dwelling place called the body and soul but we evict His spirit from our dwelling places without proper notice of eviction.

The Habitation of God

Ephesians 2:22 In whom ye also are builded together for an habitation of God through the Spirit.

The principle which identifies God's creation and purpose for us is designed to have us in a particular environment or specific location where we become like puzzle pieces all working together towards the Kingdom. Normally where the Gentiles have been viewed as set apart from the Jews by unrighteous living, the Apostle Paul's penmanship of this prison letter addresses the Gentiles to be included in the building together for a habitation of God through the Spirit. The present tense magnifies continuous and contemporaneous laboring in unity or building together with a multiplicity of materials.

The objective is to build and maintain a dwelling place for God, as He dwells in Spirit in the holy temple. As we can see, God is the Great Architect or Master Builder who properly fits His components together. The Old Testament view of this principle views God as dwelling in a place with His people while we examine the New Testament readings with the understanding that God dwells in His people. We understand now that anyone that is in Christ is a new creature. This transformation of being a new creature enables us to become a place where God can dwell.

His Dwelling is Restricted

What is your walk with Christ like? What are your actions with Christ? What is your speech with Christ? What is your work with Christ? These are all valuable questions that dwell in the world. One might consider that we invite the world to dwell in us but we evict God at each instance. God cannot dwell where we let the world dwell in us. God cannot dwell in us when we constantly have house guests dwelling within us as lustful spirits, adultery, greed, fornication, homosexuality, etc. The house tenants are not limited to when and how long they can dwell but God has to make reservations days, months, and even years out prior to taking up occupancy within us.

Is our housekeeping paid staff or on-call staff? Are the undefiled beds made or open for defilement? Are the king-size beds of iniquity advertised at a special rate versus the beds of God's grace and mercy? What are we promoting for the world to see about the one we say we have an adoration for? Are we leaving the light of Jesus on for the Spirit of God or are we pretending to be open when we are really closed for business? If we are out of order then we need to take the sign down. We need to stop advertising to God that we have a prepared place of dwelling for Him but yet no vacancies ever present themselves.

We'll prepare our physical dwellings adorning them with scriptures, crosses, and any other spiritual material means but we never adorn our temples with the same to maintain a dwelling place for God through the Spirit. Many of our spirits are so congested from large amounts of digested filth that we feed on regurgitated waste. Just the sound off that seems appalling but that's just the way we live. We live as foul servants that live out through buzzard like instincts. We don't want what's living, we only want things that have no life. We only hover around and over things that are soon to die. God is life and a great dwelling place should be preserved for Him as this is our life within Him and Him in us.

The Entrance of the Dwelling Place

How often do you take up stay in hotels or motels that do not have a presence that they are clean and provide great services? We don't even like to frequent those places that are luke-warm in servicing the public. We want the five-star or six-star treatment for the two-star or three-star payment. How strikingly we don't practice what we preach in this matter because we don't provide the same with our temples for God.

Upon entering any hotel or motel or let's just say a doctor's office, we stop at the entrance to observe the windows and what language they have on them. The language posted tells you a few things: hours of operation, what services are provided, who owns or operates the business, and what they specialize in. Our temples reflect the same when God is looking for a place of dwelling in us. God observes if our outer presence is representative of the services that are to be provided. There is no way God will enter if we have all the signs of a sin club posted on the exterior but we are claiming we have righteous habitation in the interior.

Well Prepared Dwelling Places

The work of the Trinity is constructed in a manner for all believers to be fitted and formed through the Father, the Word (Son), and the Holy Spirit that we take on His identity and provides a dwelling place for God. All the building will be perfectly fitted together in Christ to work towards the benefit of Kingdom building. God will dwell where He is welcomed and not in places where we manufacture places for Him to dwell. The painting on the walls cannot be cover and concealment facades and masquerades displaying humble places for God to dwell.

Well prepared places for God to dwell are processed through preventive maintenance. We have to prepare ourselves to be dwelling places of God through His Spirit. What we harbor in our spirits only work to take up space or a place where God can dwell. Whether we are at work, play, or during our personal time, we should assure the dwelling place of God is not compromised. Compromising the dwelling place of God will be detrimental to our well-being. We should not be present or nor shall we allow in our presence anything that will hinder us totally letting God dwell in us.

Every dwelling place of God should be sanctified for His purpose. You want a successful business, church, family, home, etc. you must sanctify it in order to ensure it will be a dwelling place for God. Lip professing will not ascertain it will be a place of God's dwelling. The growth of whatever the place is sanctioned to be relies on the growth of God's presence allowed to be manifested. Let the construction manifest

itself through God's dwelling spirit.

ABOUT THE AUTHOR

Aqeel T. Ash-Shakoor is a native of North Carolina, married with three beautiful children. Dr. Ash-Shakoor has a Bachelor of Science Degree in Business Administration from Saint Paul's College, Lawrenceville, VA; Master of Science Degree in Criminal Justice from Everest University, Tampa, Fl, and a Doctor of Philosophy Degree Human Letters, CICA International University & Seminary, Houston, TX. He is a United States Marine Corps veteran and member of Omega Psi Phi Fraternity, Inc. Dr. Ash-Shakoor authored and published his first book, "Follow the Leader (Resurrecting Men to Leadership)" in March of 2010.

Dr. Ash-Shakoor is an Ordained Minister of the Gospel of Christ. He is the Pastor of Walking With Christ Worship Center, Lansing, MI. On April 25th, 2014, Pastor Aqeel and First Lady Tanesha Ash-

Shakoor were appointed Ambassadors At-Large to the United Nations, having received Ambassadorial Appointment Letters, Doctor of Philosophy Degrees in Human Letters, Chaplaincy Licenses, and a Diploma in Chaplaincy, Leadership and Ministry from the CICA International University & Seminary. Their official titles are His Excellency Rev Dr. Aqeel and Her Excellency Rev Dr. Tanesha Ash-Shakoor, CDKA.

Dr. Aqeel T. Ash-Shakoor is the founder and CEO of Mogul NstinQ, LLC. Through this venture Dr. Ash-Shakoor authors self-help/self-improvement books, criminal justice training, diversity training, leadership training, life coaching, mentee & mentor training, motivational speaking, professional development, restorative justice training, etc.

ACKNOWLEDGEMENTS

There is no acknowledgement without first thanking my Lord and Savior Jesus Christ. I don't have to view my past because I know where He has me in my present, so I truly praise His name.

To my beautiful queen, Her Excellency Rev. Dr. Tanesha Ash-Shakoor, CDKA, words are limitless and priceless in what you have provided for me. Thank you for continuous love and support in all that we have built and are building in Jesus name. I love you and honor you. You are my Cover Girl.

I could not ask for more wonderful children than God has given me in the blessings of just being your father; Jibril, Jaylah, and Ji'Ri. You all make me who I am and give me even more purpose to keep forward progressing towards all that God has for us all. I love you all dearly!

To my parents, Henry and Evangeline Moore, you are the model for greatness in all that is parenting. When God says love, you both know how to love and love through all there is. Your guidance and support are impeccable. You keep me comforted and energized with your compassion and passion to push me forward and to never be turned around.

To each and every one of my Walking With Christ Worship Center congregation members and friends, I thank you for allowing God to direct you in my path that we may serve together in increasing the Kingdom. You know you all have a place in my heart and your pastor loves you.

To my fellow Ambassadors to the United Nations that have definitely given me honor and prophetic words of greatness, His Excellency The Right Reverend Dr. Phillip Phinn, OIA, Her Excellency Rev. Dr. Bokwey Burnley, CDKA, and His Excellency Rev. Dr.

Benson Abortogo, CDKA, your inspiration and love of the Gospel is priceless.

To a host of tremendous persons that have secured a place in my heart as we bond through Jesus to continue our servitude, I thank you all. Minister Michael Madric II, Praise Nation Ministries, you are a rising and shining star of Jesus Christ going forth to preach and teach an unapologetic and unadulterated Word of God and I support your efforts. Craig and Vera Reid (The Messenger Show, NC) for allowing me to be a special part of your vision each week delivering a word inspired by Christ; Tedrico Latham (Tedrico's Page Web Design & Video of Martinsville, VA), graphic designer for all my works, who is able to work hand-in-hand with me to craft my visions; The Parker Family of Lansing, MI (Sunday dinners are all about just that...family!); and last but not least, to each and every soul that has given me the privilege to connect with you

372

through the various forms of media and personal counseling, guidance, prayers, or acquaintances you have all been monumental in this work. Remember to "Encourage, Exhort, & Uplift!" "

"This has been your Ambassador, your Pastor's Pastor,

His Excellency Rev. Dr. Aqeel Ash-Shakoor, CDKA.

Always remember to, "Encourage, Exhort, & Uplift!

God Bless You All!"

"*Stop letting others speak into your life calling it wisdom when they don't apply the same principles to their own lives. Humbleness is not about you speaking into everyone else's life, humbleness is about realizing who you are and being transparent so others learn from your life.*""

~Dr. Aqeel Taahir Ash-Shakoor, CDKA~

BIBLIOGRAPHY

Heugens, P. R., & Scherer, A. G. (2010). When organization theory met business ethics: Toward further symbioses. *Business Ethics Quarterly*, 20(4), 643–672.

Jackson, T. (2002). The management of people across cultures: Valuing people differently. Human Resource Management 41, 4, p. 455.

Morgan, G. (2006). *Images of organization*. Thousand Oaks, CA: Sage Publications.

The Arbinger Institute. (2010). Leadership and Self-Deception: Getting Out of the Box. San Francisco, CA: Berrett-Koehler Publishers, Inc.

Thompson, J. D. (1967). Organizations in Action: Social Science Bases of Administrative Theory. New York: McGraw-Hill.

Velasquez, M. (2012). *Business ethics concepts and cases* (seventh ed.). New Jersey: Pearson Education Inc.

Woodward, J. (1965). Industrial Organization: Theory and Practice. London: Oxford University Press.